Science and the British Officer: The Early Days of the Royal United Services Institute for Defence Studies (1829-1869)

M. D. Welch

The Royal United Services Institute for Defence Studies

First Published 1998

© The Royal United Services Institute for Defence Studies

All rights reserved. No part of this publication may be reproduced, stored in a retrieval system, or transmitted in any form or by any means, electronic, mechanical, photocopying, recording or otherwise, without prior permission of the Royal United Services Institute for Defence Studies.

ISBN   0-85516-190-6
ISSN   0268-1307

The Royal United Services Institute for Defence Studies (RUSI) is an independent professional body based in London dedicated to the study, analysis and debate of issues affecting defence and international security.

Founded in 1831 by the Duke of Wellington, the RUSI is one of the most senior institutes of its kind in the world which, throughout its history, has been at the forefront of contemporary political-military thinking through debates, public and private seminars, conferences, lectures and a wide range of publications. The independence of the Institute is guaranteed by a large, worldwide membership of those people and organisations who have a serious and professional interest in the thorough and objective analysis of defence and international security.

Critical and acclaimed analysis of issues of the moment has underwritten the RUSI's Whitehall Papers for many years. Whitehall Papers are available as part of a membership package, or individually at £6.50 plus p&p (£1.00 in the UK/£2.00 overseas). Orders should be sent to the Publications Department, RUSI Whitehall, London SW1A 2ET UK and cheques made payable to the RUSI. Orders can also be made quoting credit card details (except American Express) via e-mail to: **defence@rusids.demon.co.uk**
For more details, visit our Website: www.rusi.org/rusi/

Printed in Great Britain by Sherrens Printers, Units 1 & 2, South Park, Granby Industrial Estate, Weymouth, Dorset for The Royal United United Services Institute for Defence Studies, Whitehall, London SW1A 2ET UK
Registered Charity No. 210639

CONTENTS

Preface v

Chapter 1
Introduction: Some Thoughts on Historical Research 1

Chapter 2
On the Campaign to Bring the Military and Scientific Worlds Together (1829-1857) 11

Chapter 3
Success From Crisis: The Publication of the Institution's Journal (1857-1861) 37

Chapter 4
Conclusion: First Perceptions of the American Civil War: The Structure of Victorian Military Thought (1861-1869) 58

ACKNOWLEDGEMENTS

This monograph is largely taken from the Ph.D. degree which was awarded to me in January 1998. I would like to thank the British Academy for funding this piece of research. The discussion that follows naturally reflects a great deal of what I accidentally learned as an undergraduate and postgraduate at Lancaster University. I had the great privilege of being taught by many fine lecturers across the Departments of History, Politics and Sociology. I would like to thank in particular: Prof. Preston King, Prof. John Gooch, Prof. John Hedley Brooke, Dr. Stephen Pumfrey, Dr. Stephen Constantine, Dr., Harro Höpfl, Dr. Larry Ray and Dr. Roger Smith. I would also like to thank the staff of the British Library, Lancaster University Library, Ealing Public Library, Dartford Public Library, The Trustees of Kew Garden, The British Army Museum and The Royal United Services Institute for Defence Studies. In particular at the RUSI, I would like to thank the librarian, John Montgomery, whose knowledge of the unpublished material relating to the foundation of the institution was invaluable. I would also like to thank Dr. Jonathan Eyal and Alexandra Citron.

All my family and friends supported me throughout this long journey. Two, in particular, need special mention. Having read the literature on how and how-not to gain a Ph.D., and having subsequently committed most of the sins, I fully appreciate the role of the supervisor. I was lucky to have a skilled practitioner of the art in Dr. Roger Smith, and must express my sincere gratitude to him for all his knowledge and encouragement. Finally, I owe the deepest debt of gratitude to Kirsten Nielsen, whose saintly patience and toleration enabled me to finish this project. I can only conclude with a simple thank you to you all.

Dr. Michael Welch
June 1998

PREFACE

'The writer of this, 'a well wisher' for the success of the Royal Military College and the United Service Museum, requests that the enclosed collection of papers relating to the latter may be allowed to remain in a corner of the library of the noble establishment at Sandhurst, for reference by some inquirer on a future day, anxious to know something about the origin of the Library and Museum in Middle Scotland Yard.'

J. Ford, Capt. (late 79th Regiment)
Papers Relating to the Origin and Progress of the United Service Museum (undated, but probably 1847 or 1848)

This monograph represents only the first part of a wider project undertaken by the author. As an undergraduate I was greatly interested in the historiographical section of John Keegan's *The Face of Battle* (1976). Here Keegan, it seemed, was laying down a challenge to the historian of science and ideas: how did ideas, values and beliefs affect the bloody material business of battle? Keegan himself initially seemed sceptical that such an undertaking could be successful. The history of strategic doctrine, he explained, suffered 'markedly from that weakness endemic to the study of ideas, the failure to demonstrate the connection between thought and action'. Clearly, when understood strictly, it is going to prove very difficult for any historian to establish how a set of philosophical or religious beliefs influenced a decision made by an officer some cold winters' morning in 1917! However, Keegan himself did not mean the link to be understood quite in these simple terms. While agreeing with fellow military historian, Sir Michael Howard, that military history 'must in the last resort be about battles', Keegan, also wanted to talk about a nations' 'psyche' and also asked why, when losing their own sons in battle, senior officers continued to fight 'without flinching at their posts'. Keegan called the historical approach that might answer these sorts of question 'the study of battle enlarged'. Indeed, in his demand that battles should be related 'more closely to the social context of their own times' it seems fair to conclude that Keegan was, in fact, exhorting his colleagues to consider most seriously the integration of some sort of 'history of ideas' into their discipline.

Keegan's was not a lone voice among military historians. In an important study entilted *The War Plans of the Great Powers 1880-1914* (1979), Paul Kennedy, after a careful consideration of the military, economic and political underpinnings of the war planning prior to the Great War argued that the inflexibility of the plans were 'conditioned by background attitudes'. 'The military plans', he explained, 'reflected through their inflexibilty and demand for instant action, the fatalism and determinism that was so strongly in evidence in the prevailing ideology. The social-Darwinism notions of a struggle for survival; the hyper-patriotic feelings of the military men and the 'militarised' civilians...is not all this to be witnessed in the war plans, giving them those characteristics which have appalled later critics?' For Kennedy then, like Keegan, the answer to these sorts of question would require an enlarged area for historical study, focusing 'not so much upon the military technicalities as upon the political and ideological assumptions of which they [the war plans] were an expression'.

The project, of which this monograph is a part, is therefore a response to ideas and questions already posed by these and other military specialists. It differs, however, in one very important philosophical respect. The concepts that Keegan and Kennedy put forward as being most fruitful for continued historical research miss an important centrefor ideas between the broadest social concepts and the military operations themselves. Contrary to the opinions expressed above (and wider popular opinion), the basis for the inflexibility of the military plans and the ensuing disasters of the Great War are not necessarily to be found in irrational social forces like 'fatalism'. Equally, it is not entirely satisfactory to focus on Darwin's work or some form of social

Preface

Darwinism, or for that matter on the work of Nietzsche or Hegel in the German context. Rather, the 'inflexibility', 'determinism' and the desire for 'total solutions', that Kennedy rightly detects in the war plans, owes its inheritance, paradoxically, to rationality. For the system of ideas and values that truly underpinned the war plans was the emerging ideology of positivism or Western scientific rationalism. This is the great irony that has been lost on many critics today. The disaster of the First World War was not brought about by foolish, irrational, fatalistic leaders of an unscientific military machine, but rather by optimistic believers in the age of military science and reason. It is this alternative view that the author wishes to explore.

A second observation needs to be made in this context. While military historians may know a great deal about military history (as one would expect) they are often somewhat limited, or simply disinterested, when it comes to writing about science. If a history of ideas of the sort described above is to be written, then it has to be an interdisciplinary affair. Rather than take the most simplistic and dated idea of what science or 'scientific method' may or may not be, the attempt to show the role of wider scientific values on warfare must bring the study of the history of military science in line with the modern historical study of physics, biology or the social sciences. In short, just as the Victorian hero-worshipping stories of Newton, or Darwin or the relationship between science and religion has been recast since 1960, so the traditional story of the heroes of military science must be re-examined. This brings us to the first chapter of this monograph.

While British and American military historians heaped praise on J.F.C. Fuller and Basil Liddell Hart between 1945 and 1970, they spent the early 1980s and 1990s dismantling their legend. Liddell Hart's role in the development of armoured warfare, in particular, has taken a severe pounding in recent years. However, as I demonstrate next, their views on the history of military thought and the development of what they described as 'military science' remain largely accepted by those who have deconstructed their attempts to write themselves into military history. This is a very serious omission. If Fuller is to be believed then there was little or no rational thinking about warfare, in the British context, until he addressed the problem in the 1920s and 30s. This no longer seems a reasonable position to hold. Herein lies the first challenge for the historical understanding of military knowledge in the 19th and 20th centuries. If the history of military thought or military science is longer than Fuller and Liddell Hart would allow, and doesn't progress in the rather simple manner that they imply, then a new story needs to be constructed. This would focus, as in other areas of the history of science and the social sciences, on the organisational structures put in place, the wider social influences and the methods and the goals of what constituted knowledge in the field of research at the time.

In the decades prior to 1914 the British did think they had 'scientific officers' with a rather good understanding of the future conditions of warfare, and they did think they had institutions capable of utilising this information. Candidates for such centres of activity could be the many military debating societies that sprang up, Shrivenham being one such development. The aim here, as the title suggests, has been to highlight just one, albeit a very important centre for the study of military science in the British context. Clearly, such a short volume is not going to answer all the questions posed by this programme. However, if this brief history of the RUSI prior to 1870 already convinces the reader that there is more to this matter than we have hitherto thought, then it will have done its job. For what then remains to be written is a truly convincing history of the relationship between scientific beliefs and values in the 19th and 20th century and the conduct of warfare in the same period.

CHAPTER ONE
INTRODUCTION: SOME THOUGHTS ON HISTORICAL RESEARCH

This monograph is about the early years of the modern Royal United Services Institute for Defence Studies (RUSI), its formation and the goals of its founding fathers. However, it aims to be something more than merely a paper on antiquarian interests or museumology. The intellectual 'shaping' role of the RUSI on the British army that went to war in 1914, it is suggested here, is still a significant area for academic research. This monograph, therefore, represents an invitation to historians of science and ideas as well as more 'conventional' military historians to reconsider the wider intellectual environment of the officers who held the responsibility of command in the Great War.

This call to consider the RUSI's intellectual role may seem, to some, a little unnecessary. A whole generation of military historians have already carefully considered and dissected all aspects of British Army structure prior to 1914 and have also written a vast amount of material about the personalities who fought the battles. We certainly now know far more about army reform, civil-military relations, the abolition of purchase, the staff college or the formation of the general staff than we did prior to 1960.[1] It is also the case that the military historians who have considered the varied problems of army reform in this period have been aware of the existence of the institution. As Brian Bond has observed:

> The field of military thought in the 1870s and 1880s witnessed a great outpouring of literature in Britain. The intense interest of at least a significant minority of officers in virtually every conceivable aspect of recent military history and contemporary or professional developments

can be appreciated by looking through the contents of the *Journal* of the Royal United Service Institution.[2]

Despite this fact, the need to reconsider the role of the RUSI and the wider intellectual environment is pressing. While no longer seeing the British Army as entirely dominated by inbred aristocratic cavalry officers, devoid of any interest in the well-being of their men, or in the professional conduct of warfare, one nagging doubt still lingers. These senior British officers, critics suggest, were still *fatally removed* from the progress in the worlds of science and technology going on about them. This very serious charge, in fact, has a long history and dates to the first postwar discussions of British military expertise in the 1920s and 30s. Two very famous British officers were at the centre of these discussions: J.F.C. Fuller (1878-1966) and Basil Liddell Hart (1895-1970). As early as 1926, Fuller felt that there was an obvious need for warfare to be considered more scientifically than it had been. He bluntly contrasted his own work with the intellectual desert that went before him. 'In a small way I am trying to do for war what Copernicus did for astronomy, Newton for physics, and Darwin for natural history... *My book is the first in which a writer has attempted to apply the method of science to the study of war.*'[3] This introduction, as a statement on the application of science and scientific methodology, appears to the modern historian of science and ideas as both 'grandiose' and 'absurd'.[4] But when viewed in context, Fuller's project, and the planned book of 1921, were felt to be of great importance and originality by the British military intellectuals in this period. Thus, Liddell Hart wrote encouragingly that, 'If you permit me to say so, it [the science of war concept] is the forerunner of the dawn of a new era in military thought, the product of an 'organised' brain which has hitherto been entirely lacking in all British military writing and rare even abroad'.[5]

Both men felt that science and military history would enable soldiers to learn the correct lessons of war for future military application. In *Thoughts on War* (1944) Liddell Hart, repeating a metaphor that he had first articulated some twenty years before, argued that the 'practical value of history' was 'to throw the film of the past through the mater-

Introduction: Some Thoughts on Historical Research

ial projector of the present onto the screen of the future'.[6] To this end, he felt that the scientifically-minded soldier sought to 'forecast' the future trends of warfare not in the 'imaginative flights of a Jules Verne or a H.G.Wells' but on the 'solid rock' of the 'evolutionary development of weapons'.[7] Consequently, a rational and non-fanciful prediction of these trends or evolution should be based on historical research. In *Paris, or the Future of War* (1925), Liddell Hart argued that regarding war itself as a 'hard fact' his evolutionary position was akin to that of a 'doctor called in to a sick patient'.[8] Thus, he said:

> [O]ur concern here is simply with the malady, our object being to gauge its future tendencies, in order, if possible, to limit its ravages and by scientific treatment ensure the complete recovery of the patient. As diagnosis comes before treatment, the first step is to examine the patient, estimate the gravity of his condition, and discover the seat of the trouble.[9]

For Liddell Hart, the diagnosis revolved around illustrating the failures of the pre-war military and more particularly the failure of prewar military doctrine. This doctrine he felt failed because it was nonscientific; indeed, all it really demonstrated was a 'blinkered' acceptance of Clausewitz's version of Napoleon's method. 'From 1870 to 1918', Liddell Hart explained, 'the General Staffs of the Powers were obsessed with the Napoleonic legend', and 'instead of reconnoitering the future in the light of universal history they were looking backward on a military Sodom and Gomorrah, until, like Lot's wife, they and their doctrines became petrified.'[10] In accepting that the only true objective in war was the destruction of the enemy's main force in the field, and with the construction of the mass armies that were the corollary of this objective, the generals and armies of 1914, he felt, had doomed themselves to the disasters of the Somme. Liddell Hart used this negative picture of the failure of these mass tactics deduced from Napoleon via Clausewitz, and from Clausewitz via Foch and Grandmaison to Haig, to argue that a solution to deadlock could be found in the correct use of the tank and the aeroplane. It is also well known to military historians that he found great encouragement for the fluid and 'expanding torrent' concept of infantry, and later, tank deployment, in the campaigns of General Sherman in the American Civil War and in the Mongol campaigns of the thirteenth century. This close relationship in his work between past Mongol warfare and future tank warfare was noticed by leading American military historian Jay Luvaas. He pointed out that even 'the sketch maps illustrating the campaigns of Jenghiz Khan and Sabutai... [bore] a striking resemblance to the fluid arrows used to indicate the paths of armoured columns in more recent studies'.[11] Consequently, when summarising Liddell Hart's historical approach, Luvaas observed that:

> As others drew lessons from Liddell Hart, he in turn looked to history for guidance because of its practical and philosophical value... But history does more than simply teach 'how to traverse the rugged and slippery surface of world politics without broken bones.' *History serves also as a scientific basis for theory.* Whereas Fuller, who was in many respects an intuitive man of vision, used history to teach what his own quick mind had already grasped by other methods, many of Liddell Hart's theories—particularly his views on strategy—were born of a searching examination of history... The battle of Adrianople in August, A.D. 378, had introduced the age of cavalry which had lasted until the supremacy of the horseman was ended by the longbow and pike a thousand years later. The tank attack at Amiens on August 8, 1918, struck Liddell Hart as an event of similar significance, and if modern battle conditions prohibited a reincarnation of the mounted horseman, certainly the functions of cavalry in its heyday might be appropriated by the tank. History seemed to confirm what Fuller and Liddell Hart's own theories already assumed to be true, namely that 'the action of cavalry was vital to the functioning of the body military, and when it ceased to work, warfare became stagnant.' [12]

What is of interest here is not so much showing that Fuller was more scientific than a historical Liddell Hart, but how both men in fact contrasted their scientific and historical intellectual effort with the scientific activity (if any) that went before. Instead of discussing in

Introduction: Some Thoughts on Historical Research

detail any internal theoretical problems associated with Clausewitz, as one might expect, and contrasting this critical analysis with the solutions provided by his own scientific approach, in *Paris, or the Future of War* Liddell Hart opted to popularise the idea that there was something problematic called a 'traditional military mind' barring progress in British military thinking. This mind, he felt, was antiscientific because it was 'notoriously sensitive to any breath of criticism'.[13] This seemed to imply that the military failed scientifically because they lacked what now would be called the 'open society' view of science. The claim that there was a dogmatic British military establishment closed to modern scientific speculation, like much of Liddell Hart's work, also had a lasting influence. As late as 1966, the continuing propagation of Liddell Hart's ideas in his *Memoirs Vol. 1* (1898-1938) even led two American historians of technology, T. De Gregori and O. Pi-Sunyer, to argue that:

> It was Liddell Hart's fate to understand too well and see too clearly the nature of modern war, in particular the revolutionary possibilities inherent in the internal combustion engine. At first, his military superiors failed to take... [notice] of what evidence was available; later, and in the face of growing dangers, it seems almost as if the whole military establishment was suffering from some sort of psychological disability, so encompassing was the myopia.[14]

The point of this attack on the British military is also of lasting historical relevance because the dogmatism and resistance to scientific change that frustrated Liddell Hart and Fuller in the 1920s and 1930s, as far as they were concerned applied *a fortiori* to the General Staffs on the eve of the Great War. In 'French Military Ideas Before the First World War', Liddell Hart argued that while one could, in retrospect, see that the war of 1914-18 certainly looked different to the war that the generals predicted they were going to fight, they should still be judged harshly. This was because 'the conditions that dumbfounded' them 'were only the climax of an evolutionary process which they *could* have detected'. 'Every war', argued Liddell Hart, 'for half a century, since 1861, had made it plainer.' Indeed, as 'other minds did perceive' what awaited the armies of Europe in the period prior to 1914, generals like Haig and Foch were clearly culpable.[15] In support of his critical stance Liddell Hart pointed to Jean De Bloch and a less well-known French military critic called Captain Mayer as military thinkers prior to 1914 of 'extraordinary prescience'. The key feature that sets both Bloch and Mayer apart from the generals of this period (apart from the fact that they predicted correctly the nature of a future conflict) is that they were outsiders to the established intellectual military communities. Liddell Hart observed that:

> M. Bloch, a civilian banker of Warsaw, gave a remarkably accurate diagnosis of their [recent warfares'] essential elements in his *War of the Future*, published on the eve of the twentieth century, before he had even seen the data of South Africa and Manchuria to confirm his deductions. There were also military minds, if these belonged to bodies not in the seats of authority, that foresaw the coming stalemate and pointed out its chain of causation.[16]

It is of no surprise to find the more brilliant Fuller articulating a very similar set of ideas. For example, in *Armaments and History* (1946), Fuller, while not as convinced of Bloch's foresight, certainly takes up Liddell Hart's central themes. For Fuller, the French followers of Clausewitz's version of Napoleon (Foch and Grandmaison) had abdicated all sense of military reason to a military theory that rivaled only that of the Dervishes of the Sudan for blind stupidity. He felt that the 'cult of the offensive' was not a military science but a 'piece of pure witchcraft'.[17] Like Liddell Hart, he also sought to illustrate in his 1945 book the importance of understanding the evolutionary development of weapon systems. He called his principle, illustrated by this historical survey, and 'deduced' by him from the wider laws of evolution, the 'Constant Tactical Factor'. Every weapon system, he argued, has as its goal the lessening of the danger of warfare for the user. Ultimately, however, this technological improvement is always rendered obsolete by a counter-improvement. Thus, for Fuller, the 'evolutionary pendulum of weapon power swings to and fro in pace with civil

Introduction: Some Thoughts on Historical Research

progress'.[18] Looking back on his own battle to reform the British military during the 1920s and 30s, Fuller observed sadly that the British and French General Staffs had not grasped this point and had therefore approached warfare in an 'unscientific' manner. Indeed, he also claimed that this lack of evolutionary thinking was the main weakness of Bloch's work before the Great War, arguing that even he had something of a static view of warfare.[19] What is of specific interest, however, is Fuller's linking historical criticism of the post 1918 situation and the pre-1914 world. For, much like Liddell Hart before him, Fuller has remarkably little to say about any internal theoretical difficulties faced by the followers of Clausewitz, or the theoretical, technical and historical difficulties faced by any of the scientific soldiers of the pre-war world. Indeed, while it is perfectly consistent with his own earlier pronouncements about being the Newton of military science, from the account given by Fuller in *Armaments and History* one would simply assume that such scientific officers did not even exist. Fuller, in place of such an analysis, proposes that the failure to produce scientific soldiers and therefore, by extension, any real scientific work on modern warfare prior to 1914, reflected a serious institutional shortcoming on the part of the military staffs of the European powers. This failure was that these military establishments were too far removed from the wider scientific and technological changes that were going on at the turn of the century. The failure to predict and understand the future conflict, therefore, essentially reflected this distance between the military world and the world of civil progress. Thus, Fuller says:

> These changes, as well as others resulting from scores of less prominent inventions, when coupled with strides made in the metallurgical, chemical, electrical, biological and other sciences, set in motion forces very different from those released by coal and steam... The world was in the process of sloughing its skin—mental, moral and physical—a process destined to transform the industrial revolution into a technical civilisation.
> *Divorced from civil progress soldiers could not see this.* They could not see that, because civilisation was becoming more and more technical, military power must inevitably follow suit: that the next war

7

would be as much a clash between factories and technicians as between armies and generals. (*emphasis added*) [20]

This concept of a psychologically blinkered military, divorced from civil progress in science and technology, as suggested, is still of great importance. While Fuller and Liddell Hart's reputations are not what they once were, this version of the intellectual history of British military thought prior to 1914 still lives on. Hence the real need to reconsider the role of the RUSI within the context of the actual institutional attempts to secure knowledge of future war conditions prior to 1914. That such a task is obviously necessary can be gauged from the following remarks in the very recent *Oxford History of the British Army* (1996):

> The British army developed no particular doctrine before 1914 except that of the offensive under almost all circumstances. Senior staff anticipated heavy casualties, but expected to overcome the enemy's firepower through mobility in the attack, the offensive spirit, and moral force. *Indeed there was no institution through which the army could engage in serious thinking about war before 1914*, and army manuals were often written by poorly prepared staff—thus one officer before 1914 found himself writing three manuals at once... Moreover, the traditional rivalries of cavalry, infantry, and artillery would have made an integrated doctrine very difficult to achieve even if new ideas had been adopted. In any case, it was assumed that the war would be short, lasting perhaps only six months, so that simplicity of tactics in the offensive, supported by discipline, morale, and good leadership, were really all that was required. (*emphasis added*) [21]

The point of starting to study the RUSI as an opinion shaping organisation and not simply an archive of useful information is clear. A central theoretical component of Fuller and Liddell Hart's thinking about the pre-1914 situation was the claim that the British military were fatally removed from the wider scientific world around them. This powerful argument is certainly not true and therefore hides the deeper nature of the problem. *There was never an intellectual dark age before*

Introduction: Some Thoughts on Historical Research

the Great War when the British military, as an organisation, was not very interested in what it understood to be military history, or science, and what these ideas could do for military efficiency. To deny the intellectual endeavour and the scholarly or scientific output of an organisation like the RUSI required an act of historical self-deception, which, up until this point, has effectively withstood the test of time. This monograph starts to reconsider this important point.

The officers who contributed to the Royal United Services Institute, despite their many faults, thought that they were doing more than merely producing 'literature'. The history of the institution demonstrates that the leaders and opinion shapers of the British Army were never actually divorced from the culture of science going on around them. And, despite the institution's many obvious problems, those leaders did believe that they had a thinking organ in place with which to consider the future of warfare. Indeed, the following discussion will show that the vision of a scientific army was very much on the British agenda after 1829 and was certainly not invented by the inter-war theorists. Likewise, the central idea that one should study new technology ('learning the lessons') was also invented, in the British context prior to 1870. Like many other areas of the history of science or the history of the social sciences, the replacement of the simple methodological schema of, primitive non-science - progress - enlightened science, may seem unnecessarily messy in the first instance, but it must surely prove more fruitful in the longer term.

Notes

1. See for example, H. Strachan, *Wellington's Legacy: The Reform of the British Army 1830-1854* (1984), E. M. Spiers, *The Army and Society 1815-1914* (1980), A. R. Skelly, *The Victorian Army at Home* (1977), B. Bond, *The Victorian Army and the Staff College 1854-1914* (1972), J. Gooch, *The Plans of War: The General Staff and British Military Strategy c.1900-1906* (1974), and, T.H.E. Travers, *The Killing Ground: The British Army and the Emergence of Modern Warfare 1900-1918* (1983).

2. B. Bond, *The Victorian Army and the Staff College 1854-1914* (1972), p.141.

3. Quoted in D. Pick, *War Machine: The Rationalisation of Slaughter in the Modern Age* (1993), p.165.
4. *Ibid.*, p.165.
5. Quoted in, B. Holden Reid, *J.F.C. Fuller: Military Thinker* (1987), p.81. It is also interesting to note that H.G. Wells used this kind of language of a higher brain too. See, for example, *Experiment in Autobiography* (1934) two volumes.
6. Liddell Hart, quoted in J.Wintle, *The Dictionary of War Quotations* (1989), p.122.
7. B. Liddell Hart, *Paris or The Future of War* (1925), pp. 90-91.
8. B. Liddell Hart, see for example p.79 for original use of the film metaphor.
9. *Ibid.*, p.9.
10. *Ibid.*, p.14.
11. J.Luvaas, *The Education of an Army: British Military Thought, 1815-1940* pp.396-397.
12. *Ibid.*, pp.394-395.
13. B. Liddell Hart, *op. cit.*, pp.10-11.
14. De Gregori and Pi-Sunyer, 'Technology, Traditionalism, and Military Establishments', *Technology and Culture*, 7, 1966, pp.402-407.
15. B. Liddell Hart, 'French Military Ideas before the First World War' in M. Gilbert, ed., *A Century of Conflict 1850-1950: Essays for A.J.P. Taylor* (1966), p.136.
16. B. Liddell Hart, *ibid.*, p.136.
17. Fuller, *Armaments and History: A Study of the Influence of Armament on History from the Dawn of Classical Warfare to the Second World War* (1946), p. 135.
18. *Ibid.*, p.33.
19. *Ibid.*, p.136.
20. *Ibid.*
21. T. H. E. Travers, 'The Army and the Challenge of War 1914-1918', in D. Chandler, ed. *The Oxford History of the British Army* (1996), p.213.

CHAPTER TWO
THE CAMPAIGN TO BRING THE MILITARY AND SCIENTIFIC WORLDS TOGETHER (1831-1857)

I

I am the very model of a modern major-general,
I've information vegetable, animal and mineral;
I know the kings of England, and I quote the fights historical,
From Marathon to Waterloo, in order categorical.

W.S. Gilbert, 'The Pirates of Penzance' (1879)

After the end of the Napoleonic wars in 1815, Great Britain, like all the other great powers of Europe, cut down the size of its army and navy. In the British case by far the largest part of what military capacity remained was immediately stationed abroad. This geographical distance between the British people and the bulk of her armed forces is reflected in a widespread attitude to the military organisation of this period. The British historian, Geoffrey Best, argues that this 'absence' of the Army from British soil led all too easily to 'the impression that the army after Waterloo turned into a prototype of that 'contemptible little army' about which the Kaiser was so mistaken nearly a century later'.[1] Not only is the British Army of this period seen as a pitifully small one, but the years from 1815 to 1832 are seen by military historians as a time of stagnation under an ageing Wellington and his immediate successors.

What is less well understood, however, and does not seem to fit into this image of an army struggling under autocratic leadership, is the pressure created after 1829 by a diverse group of officers to start a scientific institute. It certainly seems surprising that a fossilising army should also be an army pushing for such a potentially destabilising

Science and the British Officer

organisation. This interest in science shown by members of the Wellingtonian army has not only surprised but has looked to be something of a paradox to those few military historians who have cared to consider this question. In the best modern discussion of the history of the RUSI, the historian (and then vice president of the modern institute), Shelford Bidwell, echoing Liddell Hart and Fuller's earlier critical analysis, argued that:

> Successful armed forces can all too easily sink into authoritarianism, brooking no criticism, *rejecting any analysis of the lessons of the immediate past*, having become the mental prisoners of a successful but obsolescent technique of warfare. The great Duke himself, whose carefully contrived victories in the Peninsula had laid the foundations of the Army's traditions, was in some respects the most obdurate authoritarian ever to command British troops, the persistent opponent of every innovation except, strangely, what was to become the RUSI. (*emphasis added*) [2]

While it is the goal of this chapter to pick up the threads of this development and reconsider the history of the innovation that would become in its maturity the RUSI, it is necessary to make clear where this argument will depart from Bidwell's account of its genesis. This departure can be understood by the following two interrelated arguments. Firstly, it is entirely accepted that the later members of the RUSI sought to learn the 'lessons of the immediate past' as Bidwell quite rightly suggests. This was the main scientific activity and function of the institute prior to 1914. *However, it is not the case that the founders of the original United Service Museum (USM) had this particular version of military science as their prime concern in 1829.* In fact, the idea of science held by the founders of the earlier institute had altogether different and broader connotations than merely studying military history for some future use. This broader interest in science, and what it could do for the British military, was an expression of cultural values widely held in British society at the time. This chapter, therefore, will seek to demonstrate that, while a British military interest in science seems hard to grasp from a modern perspective, the activity carried out by these officers after 1830 mirrors almost perfectly what historians of science have discovered about the social and geographical bases for the development of British science in the early nineteenth century. Secondly, and more importantly in the context of this thesis, if it is the case that the scientific institute of the British military in 1830 did not have as its prime goal the task it had in 1914, learning valid military lessons for future use, then it follows that the intellectual activity of learning the lessons of military history itself was nurtured, developed and has a history. This crucial development in British military thought is also locked into the story of RUSI.

II

The initial momentum for the 'innovation' that would ultimately crystallise into the USM was the result of a ground-swell of opinion among a diverse group of army and navy officers. Reflecting on this popular desire for science to enter the military profession, the 1931 historian of the RUSI, Capt. E. Altham, observed that 'the foundation of the Royal United Service Institution, like that of most great projects, seems to have been due to the enterprise of a few in uniting and giving effect to a considerable body of opinion, rather than the inspiration of any particular individual'.[3] Both Altham and Bidwell agree that the catalyst for this constructive activity in 1830-31 was an article in *Colburn's United Service Journal* in February of 1829. In this journal (not to be confused with the journal of RUSI, first published in 1857), a correspondent signing himself as 'An old Egyptian Campaigner' wrote:

> [M]y proposal is that to give *a tone of science to the character of both services*, it would be a desirable point to set on foot a Museum, to be formed, conducted and maintained, solely by the military, medical and civil branches of the Royal Navy, the King's Army, the Hon. East India Company's services and their connections: to be called the United Service Museum, if patronised by His Gracious Majesty, as the head of the Army, by his R.H. the Duke of Clarence, the actual heads of the Navy, would soon attain an interesting character, reflecting honour on the nation, raising in public estimation the individual contributors to and supporters of it, and finally proving that the two professions have

entered the lists of science, and are ready to contend for honours 'Tam Artibus quam Armis'. *(emphasis added)* [4]

In May 1831, a prospectus was issued explaining that the intention of the proposed Museum was to act as a general depot for works of art, natural history, arms and armour and 'plans and models connected with the pursuits of the Naval and Military Professions'.[5] It is clear that the Museum was, from the very beginning, only one aspect of a much larger and more ambitious institution. The prospectus goes on to inform potential subscribers that it would 'also comprise a Library, with books of reference in general Science and Art, and on professional subjects in particular... It is also contemplated to introduce Lectures on suitable subjects, to be delivered... by competent Members of the two Professions; and to be illustrated, when necessary, by experimental apparatus; the latter to form an item of the Establishment.'[6] Indeed, the subscriber is left in no doubt about what his ten shillings annual subscription might buy:

> The United Service Museum is intended to be *strictly a scientific and professional Society, not a Club.* The chief aim of the Institution is to foster the desire of useful knowledge amongst the members of the United Service, and to facilitate its acquisition *at the least individual or public cost. (emphasis added)* [7]

By July 1831, and with 950 subscribers behind them, the newly formed provisional committee of the 'Naval and Military Library and Museum', now meeting at the then fashionable Thatched House Tavern in St James Street, London, had taken the opportunity to reformulate their objectives in more detail. While repeating their three main practical aims, the circular of this month also alludes to, and expounds upon, the wider social goals of the proposed institute. The opening paragraph stated:

> Whilst other professions have establishments in which their members may prosecute the studies which their particular objects require, and find facilities for the acquisition of general knowledge and useful

information, according to the actual state and progress of science, the improvements of art, and the changes or modifications which are continually taking place in the practice of all professions, the Naval and Military Services, though affording peculiar facilities for the formation of such an establishment, and greatly susceptible of being benefited by it, have provided no institution in which their members, when not actively employed, may improve, through their own exertions, the special, elementary education which they may have originally received.[8]

This particular formulation of the institute's goal was felt to be very important. It reflected the desire by a leading advocate and founder member of the USM, Major-General Sir Henry Hardinge (1785-1856, Viscount, Commander-in-Chief 1852-55 and Field Marshal in 1855), to emphasise that 'the object of the Institution was not confined to making a collection of interesting exhibits' but reflected the original idea as he understood it, that the institute was to actively encourage 'the study and advancement of professional knowledge'.[9] It was, however, the more public aspects of the institution, rather than the advancement of Hardinge's 'professional knowledge', that initially attracted most attention. By August 1831, the flood of book donations and objects of natural history that would periodically threatened to overwhelm the newly appointed officers of the USM had already started to arrive at the museum's premises in Whitehall Yard. A brief summary of a mere fraction of these early donations gives a flavour of the sort of eclectic material that would continue to come over the course of the next twenty-five years. For example, for the Library came:

> Locke's *Life and Correspondence*, 2 vols.
> *Letters on England*, 2 vols.
> Hunt's *Byron and Some of his Contemporaries*
> Hazlitt's *Conversations of James Northcote*
> Antommarchi's *Memoirs of the Last Two Years of Napoleon's Exile*
> Beauchamp's *Narrative of the Invasion of France in 1814 and 1815*, 2 vols.
> Prince Eugene's *Memoirs*

The Military Sketch Book , 2 vols.

For the Museum came:

> By Capt. W.H. Smyth RN an extensive Collection, consisting of Geology and Mineralogy, topographically arranged, and including a complete series of the productions of Vesuvius, lavas of Etna, Stromboli, and other Volcanoes. Also a diversified series of specimens of Antiquity, and Miscellaneous Articles from various parts of the world.
>
> By Commander Downe a Collection. Sixty cases of Stuffed Birds, Quadrupeds, and Fishes, a Cabinet of Entomological Specimens from Western Africa, War-like Instruments, Shells, dried Ferns from Fernando Po, and Curiosities from all Quarters of the Globe.
>
> By Capt. W. Tower, 3rd Foot, Shells, Boar Spear, and a variety of Curiosities from India.
>
> By Lieut. Gen. Sir Herbert Taylor, GCH some Bird Skins from Ascension, and a stuffed Black Monkey.
>
> By Capt. W.F. Owen, RN a Shark's Jaw, out of the body of which was taken the mutilated remains of a little boy which it had seized the day before whilst bathing at Fernando Po; a three horned Chameleon, and four snakes in spirits; some shells, new specimens, from Fernado Po.
>
> By Rev. L. Bridge the Skeleton of a small Turtle.

And finally, for a proposed 'model room' came:

> By Dr. James Boyle, RN Model of a Schooner made by Natives in the Interior of Western Africa, with rudely carved figures representing a band playing.

The Campaign to Bring the Military and Scientific Worlds Together

By Commander Lihou, RN Model of a rudder invented by himself, which, by an order issued by the Commissioners of the Navy, all men-of-war are to be fitted with.

By Messrs. Gordon, Civil Engineers and Mechanists. Capt. Phillips's Capstan with the latest Improvements; a Chain Messenger invented by Mr G.; Specimen of the Manchester and Liverpool Rail; a Brass Six-Pounder on Capt. Marshall's improved construction.

By Captain Norton. Model of the Rifle Percussion Shell, his own invention. Model of a Fire-Arrow of his own invention, to be discharged from a rifle, the advantages of which are accuracy of direction and increased range, attained by the spin given to it by the Rifle; also a hollow Ball for a Rifle, containing its own charge, his own invention.[10]

This flood of donations to the museum was facilitated by the free passage of items on British government transports, and in 1834, the setting up of 'Local committees' in Chatham, Deal, Dublin and Edinburgh and in more far flung places over the Empire such as Ceylon, Madras, Kingston and Port Royal in Jamaica, and Quebec. Indeed, so successful was this part of the campaign that by 1858 the view was expressed by the council of the institute that the premises at Whitehall Yard, London, could no longer cope with the range and sheer quantity of the donations still arriving. A short amendment on the changing criteria for the collection politely reminded contributors that, 'Large stuffed animals' could no longer be accepted 'unless they have some connection with a military operation.'[11]

While the rapid 'internationalisation' of the project noted above is very impressive, it is the underlying division between an interest in eclectic natural history and technology and the advancement of something called 'professional knowledge' that attracts attention. On the one hand, it is clear from the literature that some early advocates, such as Hardinge, had a deep long-term vision for the institute, while support-

17

ers, such as its first secretary, Commander Downes RN, were more interested in looking for a permanent home for their collections of natural history. This intellectual diversity has alarmed somewhat those scholars who have observed a parallel interest in North America at precisely the same time. In *The Soldier and the State* (1957), the leading American political scientist, S. P. Huntington, noticed that there was something called a 'Military Enlightenment in the South' between 1832 and 1846. The military societies that sprang into being led only 'brief but active lives'. '[T]he Enlightenment', he continued, 'was not entirely divorced from technicism and... was rather closely linked to the intellectual currents of the day... The military journals generally had more technical articles than professional ones on the art of war. A military society, such as the United States Naval Lyceum founded by officers at the Brooklyn Naval Yard in 1833, sponsored scientific and technical researches and, at times, seemed more preoccupied with meteorology, zoology, botany, and mineralogy, than with more strictly naval subjects.'[12] How these seemingly diverse objectives could have been drawn so easily together by the British officers needs to be understood, not in purely military terms, but against the backdrop painted by historians of science.

III

The beginning of the nineteenth century is seen as the starting point for an extraordinary burst of intellectual activity. The progress being made across many fields of the natural sciences was followed with great interest and excitement by large numbers of people from a variety of social strata. The social historian, F R Klingender, observed that 'the first thirty years of the nineteenth century were the critical period of the industrial revolution'. Reflecting on the wide social interest associated with these scientific and technological changes he added that:

> [I]t is probably true that so broad a section of the English middle class has never again been so genuinely interested in science as in the early nineteenth century. The provincial philosophical societies multiplied rapidly, and the best of them became centres where the most important

The Campaign to Bring the Military and Scientific Worlds Together

research of the period was undertaken... People all over Britain followed John Dalton, Sir Humphry Davy and Michael Faraday as they made their epoch-advances in atomic theory and electro-chemistry. Thousands of amateur scientists formed an appreciative public for the astronomical discoveries of Sir William Herschel and of his son, Sir John, or for the restatement of geology by Sir Charles Lyell. By 1830 the ground had been prepared for the two great achievements of nineteenth century science, the theory of thermodynamics, and that of evolution by natural selection.[13]

The multiplication of the Literary and Philosophical societies (henceforth Lit and Phil) in the newly industrialised cities and factory towns was closely associated with this first phase of the industrial revolution. Such bodies were set up in: Manchester (1781), Derby (1783), Newcastle upon Tyne (1793), Birmingham (1800), Glasgow (1802), Liverpool (1812), Plymouth (1812), Leeds (1818), Cork (1819), York (1822), Sheffield (1822), Whitby (1822), Hull (1822) and Bristol (1823).[14] Sometimes seen as merely fashionable clubs for wealthy merchants or mill owners, many Lit and Phils were, as in the case of Manchester's under the leadership of John Dalton (1766-1844), important locations for the initial propagation of scientific values and research. Even when they undertook no serious scientific research of their own, as the smaller bodies often did not, the local society still served as a useful mechanism for supplying 'popular science' lectures and the 'air pump' type of scientific entertainment captured for us by artists like Joseph Wright of Derby (1734-1797).

After the mid-1820s there was a decline in the formation of new regional Lit and Phil societies. Historians of science, however, have been very interested by the emergence of the scientific 'peripatetic associations' like 'The Union of Mechanics Institutes', (UMI) founded in 1837, and 'The British Association for the Advancement of Science' (BAAS) founded at a meeting in York in 1832. The BAAS is of particular interest as its formation is most closely associated with the articulation of fears about the failure of British science to keep up with German scientific organisations. The most notable voice among those members of the BAAS warning of the dangers of British science falling behind the rest of Europe was that of Charles Babbage (1792-1871) in his *Reflections on the Decline of Science in England* published in 1830. Closely related to the ultimate success of these calls for a more professional approach to the whole scientific enterprise in England, historians of science have also observed a shift away from the more regional structure of British science described above to a more 'metropolitan' one after 1830. This structural relocation is associated with the emergence of London as the centre of British science, and the rise of the single subject 'disciplinary societies'.[15]

Given the transitional state of British science described above, it is hardly surprising that the USM should have among its founders individuals who emphasised the naturalist aspect of scientific activity. Their enthusiasm for the new museum reflects the older, amateur scientific values of the Lit and Phil societies and the continued flourishing of the 'natural history movement' in Great Britain throughout the 1830s and 1840s. That relatively wealthy, often quite senior officers should have understood the intellectual goal of their institute in this light emphasises the popularity of these scientific organisations among the social classes that many soldiers were drawn from. No matter how derivative the plan was, these supporters of the proposed institute did have a highly original purpose for this popular form of science. The practical goal these founders aimed at, as the old Egyptian campaigner first stated, was to give the officers of the British armed forces an impressive and prestigious national stage. As the proposals and the list of exhibits testify, the institute was clearly meant to be something more than an enlarged regimental or corps museum (some supporters had been impressed by a French artillery museum in Paris). Based in the heart of London, the USM was envisaged as the ideal mechanism for displaying the scientific work undertaken by the many able scientific collectors found among the services. Although this particular 19th century 'character' was later lampooned by Gilbert in his operetta, the institute represented the first bold attempt by the British military to associate, in the minds of the general public, an image of the officer with the cultured image of the natural philosopher. While this ambition therefore marks an important and novel shift from a simple regional interest in natural history to a national one by a profession whose intellect, even before the debâcle of the Crimean War, was traditionally underrated, two basic conclusions need to be underscored. Firstly, the 'gifts' to the proposed library and museum of the USM clearly betray the inheritance of the provincial Lit and Phils. C.A. Russell, in *Science and Social Change* (1983), notes that Bedford's 'Reading Room Society' formed in 1826 'commenced its existence by ordering the *Quarterly* and *Edinburgh Reviews*. The first books recorded in this library were a copy of Linnaeus, one of Gilbert's *Fundamentorum Botanicorum pars Prima* and an edition of *Don Quixote*'.[16] As the founding of Bedford's society therefore illustrates, what the officers and original donors saw as suitable material for their library was essentially identical to the wide-ranging literature the founders of many other Lit and Phil societies also saw as suitable. Secondly, just as the reading material of the USM shared the vision of a good library held by many Lit and Phils, so the membership's vision of the display of the exhibits of geology, botany and ornithology shared the contemporary vision of good natural history.

Many natural history clubs and field societies had embryo museums displaying their work. How high the quality of the collections to be deposited at the USM were, when compared to the work undertaken by a regional group like, for example, the Newcastle Natural History Society, is no longer possible to judge (the collections donated having long since been broken up). However, the initial motivation and reasons for officers joining in the widespread enthusiasm for collecting natural history was probably much the same as anyone else's at the time. To explain the reason for alighting on natural history in the 19th century, Russell argues convincingly that 'without doubt a genuine spirit of scientific enquiry moved in many naturalists whose collecting instincts had been brought properly under control'.

> These men were nearly all amateurs, and such was the state of the art that an amateur could very well pursue it. Mathematical expertise was unnecessary; experimental technique, though important, could be

learned on one's own; no lengthy laboratory courses were necessary; and the intellectual demands, though considerable, were not impossible to meet. The feverish pursuit of natural history occupied many a lone amateur as he burned the midnight oil, classifying, mounting his specimens to his own satisfaction.[17]

The underlying affinity between the older Lit and Phils and the emerging USM is also illustrated by a striking relationship between the architectural specifications of the new building proposed in London and the older regional structures. In their demand that their planned institute include a museum, a lecture theatre and a library, the founders of the USM were copying the internal features of buildings belonging to the larger Lit and Phil societies. Understood in the light of the continued influence of Francis Bacon's thought in England, the internal structure of the proposed USM building, like that of the older Lit and Phils corresponds very closely to the description of a 'research establishment' found in the account of 'Solomon's House' given in the highly readable *New Atlantis* (1627) (Francis Bacon, Viscount St Albans, 1561-1626, also see, *Novum Organum* 1620).[18] This Baconian conception, first incorporated into the design of The Royal Society of London, certainly had a lasting regional influence. As late as the 18th and early 19th centuries, Russell observed that underlying the deep stress placed on amateur science in Britain 'lay the philosophy of Baconianism... [which] permeated so much of the Lit and Phil movement, especially in northern England'.[19] The historian of ideas, Anthony Quinton, has also suggested that this aspect of this popular work of utopian fiction remained 'one of the most influential aspects of Bacon's thinking about science', arguing that the real historical interest of Solomon's house lay in its 'allocation of its personnel to particular tasks in a co-operative undertaking'.[20]

The Baconian notion of scientific workers going off to collect facts for a central institute, as a conception of scientific enterprise, had clear benefits for these founders of the USM. The most obvious attraction of copying the older institutional structure for the founders was the fact

The Campaign to Bring the Military and Scientific Worlds Together

that it signalled to potential supporters, probably already aquainted with Bacon's work and the Lit and Phil movement, the sorts of scientific activity they could expect the new institute to carry out.[21] But most importantly, the attraction of natural history as a branch of science to a future membership, composed of serving British officers, would be that it was one of the few scientific disciplines which travel, and the inevitable stationing overseas encouraged rather than impeded. The self-taught officer could practice his discipline with a few portable instruments and return his findings to the institute in London, no matter where he was stationed in the Empire. Indeed, the long tours of duty in the more remote parts of the Empire made such botany and geology even more important, and the officers that carried it out, in turn, all the more scientifically worthy.

There is no need to press these suggestions about the close affinities between the USM and the older Lit and Phil movement and Baconianism any further. The discussion above shows that even the oddities or defects of this aspect of the military project are not due to the founders of the USM having particularly poor minds or even having particularly eccentric views as to what science entailed. This picture starts to illustrate the fact that, far from being removed from the trends of intellectual society around them, even this most eclectic aspect of the early Institute was firmly rooted in the traditions and institutions of the scientific enterprise of the time.

The observation that the collection of objects of natural history was understandable given the social and educational circumstances of many British officers is only a first step in a more sympathetic understanding of the foundation of the USM. What Hardinge and his supporters understood by the 'professional officer', and how this idea related to a scientific institute bent on being more than just a home for exhibits of natural history is far more important. The next section will argue that this particular group's desire to bring the world of the military professions and science together was intimately tied to the emergence of London as a centre for British science after 1830.

IV

The possible sources of scientific knowledge and entertainment for the officer in London were large and continued to grow after 1830. London served as a focus for a renewed interest in higher education after 1815. The concrete manifestation of this interest, along with an overall increase in the number of professorships in science, can be witnessed by the founding of University College London in 1826 and King's College London in 1828. Side by side with this boost to academic research came a deluge of periodicals mixing literary, musical and scientific subjects. The historian Robert Altick has pointed out that 1824 was something of a boom year, which saw the establishment of the *Quarterly Review*, the *Westminster Review* and *Blackwood's Magazine*.[22] In a similar vein, London became a magnet for many scientists attempting make a reputation for themselves. As Ian Inkster and Jack Morrell say:

> London social life included what might be styled scientific attractions, some profound and some simply silly, where the vague line between scientist (itself a word coined only in 1833) and laymen might vanish altogether, or where the scientist could show off his wares to an admiring laity: the Thames Tunnel (1828), balloon ascents, Professor Wheatstone's telegraphic device at King's College, Professor Owen's bones at the College of Surgeons, Herschel's great telescope at Slough, Babbage's calculating machines, a whale stranded in the Thames, or the corpse of Jeremy Bentham, publicly dissected by Southwood Smith.[23]

London also provided more serious intellectual 'sustenance' for those gentlemen of leisure who pursued scientific matters.[24] The range of scientific institutes providing lectures like the Royal Institution (1799), the Russell Institution (1808), and the Philosophical Society of London (1811) were joined by a large number of more narrowly defined 'disciplinary societies':

The Campaign to Bring the Military and Scientific Worlds Together

The Linnean Society (1788)
The Mineralogical Society (1799)
The Chalcographic Society (1803)
The Geological Society (1807)
The Astronomical Society (1820)
The Meteorological Society (1823)
The Zoological Society (1826)
The Geographical Society (1830)
The Entomological Society (1833)
The Botanical Society (1836)
The Microscopical Society (1839)
The Pharmaceutical Society (1841)
The Chemical Society (1841)
The Physical Society (1874). [25]

The aims of these new specialists, it has been argued, were, firstly, to demarcate their scientific activity from other 'culturally prestigious activities' such as music or the arts.[26] Secondly, each organisation sought to improve communications between workers in the field, define problems, and decide for themselves what areas they ought to be following rather than allow any higher general organisation, like the Royal Society, to decide the matter. Finally, the members of these new scientific disciplines sought to forge new pathways and career structures for themselves within the changing university system. While this broad outline can essentially be understood as the modern criteria for the professional status of university trained scientists in this country, two specific issues are relevant to a British military perception of this change in the 1830s and 40s. Firstly, early single subject organisations did not conform perfectly to the model of scientific development described above. The Geological Society, for one, did not simply emerge to push for a recognition of the utility of the discipline in industrial concerns like mining or for more university chairs in the subject. The leading British historian of science, Roy Porter, has argued that none of the leaders of this scientific body, bar one, actually had any involvement with the practical industrial applications of geology in the first dozen years of the 19th century. Many leading figures in applied geology remained outside the organisation. Indeed, according to the papers of its first President, G. B. Greenough, it began as a gentlemen's dining club charging fifteen shillings for the pleasure of attending. As Russell says:

> In these circumstances, Porter feels not that utility was necessarily a 'false banner' for the Geological Society, but rather that it was a concept more comprehensive than mere technical applicability, embracing 'intellectual, religious and moral benefits quite as powerfully as material advantage'. In other words, it had the same broad cultural overtones as in the contemporary Literary and Philosophical Societies.[27]

The USM, like the Geology Society, emerged rapidly from a dining club in London's fashionable taverns. Indeed, as late as 1857, leaders of the military institute specifically referred to the perceived success of the Geological Society. In his Chairman's Address of 1857, Col. The Hon, James Lindsay MP (1815-1874) observed that

> '...all other professions have establishments for imparting professional knowledge and general information. In the learned and scientific societies of the country, naval and military science has been hitherto unrepresented and unrecognised; it is the province of this Institution to fill that vacancy and become to the services what the museum in Jermyn Street is to geology and that of Kew is to botany.'[28]

Porter's idea of an embracing moral conception is, therefore, directly relevant here. While Hardinge had spoken of a professional officer, his association of the idea with the ideal of science was still closely related to his own understanding of these wider intellectual and moral aspects of the activity. Indeed, a simple facet of the scientists' own push to achieve a 'professional' status will make this clear. In 1799 Sir Humprey Davy (1778-1829, see, *Elements of Chemical Philosophy* 1812) could write that 'philosophy, chemistry and medicine' were his 'profession' because he was paid to carry out his scientific research. Clearly, in this narrow sense of the term, soldiers and sailors, despite the continuation of the system of purchase within the Army, were members of 'professions' in the same sense that members of the law and the clergy were. Thus, the desire to be seen as 'professional' by British officers at this time was not quite the same project that members of the BAAS, like Babbage, were themselves engaged in.

Ironically, the new scientists wished to have something of the order and seeming permanence of the old professions, while the Army wished to have some of the wider prestige of the emerging disciplines. To understand more fully the attraction of science to Hardinge and his supporters at this time, we have therefore to move from modern worries about what the term 'profession' might mean or has come to mean, and consider in context what functions and goals these officers thought a military version of Solomon's house ought to carry out, and detail what deeper moral undercurrents drove their particular vision.

V

The expansion of the museum provided advocates of the institute like Downes with a satisfactory home for their collections of birds and animals. From August 1831 onwards, however, what the USM would actually do to promote professional scientific progress in the services became, quite properly, the central practical problem for the supporters of Hardinge. Three main approaches were put forward by this group at the annual 'report to the committee'. Firstly, the idea was proposed that the institute was to become an independent scientific board, to which fellow officers would be encouraged to bring their latest scientific inventions. Advocates of this approach argued that:

> [T]he facilities which the Institution will afford to those officers who labour for the Improvement of the Arts and Sciences more immediately applicable to their own professions, in bringing their inventions, either by models, drawings, or descriptions, under the eyes of those persons who are most capable of appreciating them... many excellent inventions had been lost to the state from the impossibility of compe-

tent judges being made acquainted with their merits. The Navy Board are inundated with such, and have not the leisure to attend to them all. In this Institution we have a remedy for those evils; every invention can now be submitted to every member of the profession, and its merits justly appreciated; and I have no doubt that the public Boards will do every thing in their power to support so valuable an institution. [29]

This idea seems to have been the brain-child of those who saw a more political and procurement orientated role for the USM located between the Army and Navy and the organs of government. Later advocates of this role abandoned the idea of addressing the issue directly to the Admiralty (whose views on the subject are not on record) and proposed instead a closer relationship between the institute and the Committees of the House of Commons. Closely related to the more traditional Baconian structure of the Lit and Phil society, it was argued that the institute should also become a centre for scientific information and research. To forward this goal, and further establish credible scientific ties, the 'Transactions of the Royal Society' (from 1830) were added to its growing list of continental military publications. In 1836 the council also informed the members that from that year onwards a 'Meteorological Journal' would be kept at the institute and invited officers making scientific journeys to 'compare their barometers with that of the Institution', which, they claimed, was a brand new instrument 'of the best construction'.[30]

The final approach sought to emphasise the educational role of the USM. This idea focused on the transmission, by public lecture, of the latest scientific practices relevant to the military profession to the wider Army and Navy. This conception of the role of the institute was voiced as soon as the building in Scotland Yard, Whitehall was obtained in 1833. The effort resulted in the delivery in the following year of a series of three lectures by Rev. D. Lardner FRS, 'On Steam Connection with India', the Rev W. Ritchie FRS., 'On the Principles of Experimental Philosophy Applied to Engineering' and W.S. Harris FRS, 'On the Defence of Ships and Buildings from Lightening'.[31] This feature reflects the importance of the seasonal lecture in London scientific life after 1830. Indeed, while no longer considered to be in the 'first rank', figures like Lardner and Ritchie are well known to historians of science. As Inkster and Morrell explain: 'A Scottish divine, William Ritchie (1790 -1837) was for seven years a dominant London lecturing personality. He began lecturing on the physical sciences at the Royal Institution in 1830 and was regularly employed there until his death, retained as a professor but paid on a per lecture basis which brought him between £50 and £80 annually.'[32] Dionysius Lardner supplemented his income as professor of natural philosophy at University College with widespread lecturing and writing after leaving his chair in 1829.

The choice of having these leading figures of the London circuit clearly demonstrates the commitment to the idea that the USM should be seen on the same prestigious social level as the Royal Institution or Russell Institution. The selection of these prominent figures of the London circuit also provides an important clue to the scientific content of the institute. With their large work load, Ritchie and others tended to give derivative lectures whenever they could. The subject matter of the USM series seems to be an example of stock material being given a specific technological spin. It can be seen, therefore, that this series of lectures, and later ones given by the institute in Scotland Yard, do not exhibit the specific scientific and historical concerns of the mature organisation described by modern military historians like Bidwell. Although a lecture, in 1837 was given by a Lt. John Goodwin on 'The Importance and Utility of the Study of History, as Connected with the Naval and Military Professions', the demand that one should derive lessons for future military use from such historical work does not figure as a significant subject for the lecture programmes.[33] Indeed, when one delves deeper and considers one of the very few early philosophical or methodological pronouncements on what science might actually mean to the future of the military professions, it is clear that its possibilities were initially understood in a very restricted sense. In a discussion of who ought to be employed to give the institute's expert lectures, it was argued that:

> [T]he sciences immediately connected with the Professions are the Mechanical Sciences, or those which relate to Natural Philosophy, and depend on the operation of Physical Forces... It is important here to remark the distinction between those Sciences, and others of which the connection with the Professions is less intimate: for, generally speaking, the points in which the laws of Nature apply in the exercises of the Professions, are in matters regarding the effects produced, rather than the component elements of the agents which we employ. Thus, for example, when we employ as efficient forces, wind, water, or gunpowder, our business is in general immediately with the effects produced, and remotely with the constituent parts or chemical analysis of the substances employed.[34]

This methodological statement is typical of the period. It can clearly be read as an exhortation to study only the practical consequences of specific phenomena rather than to produce a more general theoretical system of ideas.[35] Altick described this recognisable concern as an interest 'concentrated upon physical properties and processes rather than the abstract truths which underlay them'.[36] This methodological pronouncement also makes perfectly clear the very narrow level of scientific analysis—the elucidation of efficient causes—that the membership of the USM initially had in mind.

Herein lies the final key to the paradox observed by Bidwell. Historically, the British Army, as personified by Wellington, did not feel it was fundamentally challenged by this version of science and technology in the late 1820s and 1830s. As the leading British military historian John Keegan tells us, the great Duke himself was 'musical, and deeply interested by mechanics and astronomy'.[37] More importantly in military terms, the basic conception of a 'Wellingtonian system of warfare', as understood and practised by the British Army at Waterloo in 1815, was seen to be the near perfect outcome of a long tradition of military practice and not merely some new departure point. Science at the narrow level described above could be openly welcomed, for interpreted in this restricted manner, it did not seem to the members of the USM, or probably to Wellington himself, to threaten an obviously successful system of tactics, organisation and weaponry. It must be emphasised, therefore, that the contemporary military feeling towards this scientific activity was not the modern fear of rapid technological change—for this theme does not occur in the literature—but enthusiasm for the interesting scientific 'novelties' that might bring to perfection this pre-existing British military system.

Given this essentially conservative interpretation of what history, science and technology might do for the British military in the 1830s and 40s, it will be fruitful to consider the internal military context for the promotion of scientific activity by the USM. As suggested, all the early members were perfectly clear on the desirability to show that the British military had *entered the lists of science*, and to give the forces of the crown the *tone and character of science*. For this public image to succeed, as we have also seen, the members of the USM did not feel that they had to convince the public that they had a 'theory of war' in the sense that the natural scientist had, for example, Newton's 'theory of universal gravitation'. Nor can this attempt to convince the public that the British military had a scientific body of some national standing be simply understood as a cynical attempt at public relations. Clearly, it was an attempt to raise the value of the Army's traditionally low public estimation by being seen to be involved with a social project then held in high regard. Nevertheless, there was a deeper internal moral project, understood in Porter's sense of the term, associated with the formation of the institute. Indeed, this moral dimension of science was understood by the members of the USM to be one of the most important and desirable aspects of the whole enterprise.

It is well known to military historians that commanders of the British Army at this time had expressed dissatisfaction with the level of professional competence among significant numbers of their officers. Wellington himself, as Keegan points out in *The Mask of Command* (1987), was forced to carry out an excessively large amount of work due partly to there being few capable staff officers available to him, and he had real difficulty in removing ineffective officers at command level.[38] As Bond notes in *The Victorian Army and Staff College,*

Hardinge himself had, in fact, been one of the few outstanding staff officers. In this military context, the advocates of the formation of a scientific institute implied that their scientific institution would be of vital importance as it would, ultimately, raise the general level of British military efficiency. It was felt that a sound knowledge of science would instil a determination among the next generation of officers to fulfil their professional obligations more fully than had hitherto been the case. Thus, these soldiers expected that the scientific officer of the future would also be the diligent professional officer of the future.

What the proponents of the USM therefore found morally desirable about scientific knowledge was that it was a form of useful knowledge to be gained, to paraphrase Wordsworth's view, 'only... slowly and with difficulty'.[39] This acquisition of difficult higher knowledge by junior officers would, it was hoped, distract them from the more unproductive pursuits of the young men traditionally attracted to the British officer corps. In this desire the older officers at the USM wholeheartedly agreed with and adopted for their own goals a wider social purpose for scientific learning proposed by Humphry Davy. Davy, for example, had recommended the pursuit of amateur scientific investigation to gentlemen because, he said, it 'may become a source of consolation and of happiness in those moments of solitude' and 'it may destroy diseases of the imagination, owing to a deep sensibility; and it may attach the affection to objects, permanent, important, and ultimately related to the interest of the human species'.[40] Morrell and Thackray have observed that this 'source of consolation' was, on occasion, specifically aimed at officers of Davy's aquaintance. As they say, 'possible claimants to the title of men of knowledge increased markedly in the years after the Napoleonic Wars. Their number included army officers retired on half pay and looking for suitable diversion: witness Roderick Impey Murchison (Sir Roderick Impey Murchison 1791-1871, see, *The Silurian System* 1839), whom Sir Humphry Davy encouraged to leave off grouse shooting and 'set to' at science.'[41] Members of the USM hoped that it was possible that officers involved with such a profound activity would, as one writer put it, 'detach many of our friends from the club-house and the billiard-table'.[42] Or, as another put it more bluntly: '[A]bove all, it [the institute]', he felt, 'will eminently tend to wean the minds of many a gallant officer from idleness and dissipation, by placing before him examples of rational pursuit, and by furnishing him with new objects to win his attention as well as new motives to change his career.'[43] Scientifically committed officers of the old order, like Hardinge, were therefore proposing an enlightened military-social *quid pro quo* arrangement. Science was to be enriched by the contribution of the many able amateur scientists to be found among the British officer corps. Likewise, the scientific enterprise would be aided by the costs of this extra work being met out of the private pocket of the military institution (or in the case of Kew and the transport costs of the USM, out of Admiralty funds). From the British military's point of view, involvement with a project held so highly in the esteem of an increasingly important social class was valuable in itself. More importantly, the Army would ultimately benefit directly by the expected contribution scientific officers would make to its overall efficiency in wartime.

The conclusion that one must draw from this arrangement is not that these officers were necessarily absurd in their ambition. Highly, and to our modern eyes perhaps overly optimistic, yes, but certainly not removed from the wider intellectual and scientific trends of their time. Having established, sympathetically, this more complex starting point for a British military involvement with science, it will now be possible to consider its success and failures once the original inspiration and enthusiasm for the project were confronted by more concrete social, institutional and methodological difficulties.

Notes

1. G. Best, *War and Society in Revolutionary Europe, 1770-1870* (1982), p.231.
2. S. Bidwell, 'The Royal United Services Institute for Defence Studies 1831-1991' *RUSI Journal*, Summer 1991, p.69.

3. E. Altham, *One Hundred Years of the Fighting Services: The Centenary of the Royal United Service Institution 1831-1931* (1931), p.1.
4. *Ibid.*, p.1. (For what it is worth, 'Tam artibus quam armis', 'As much through the arts as through weapons', needs to be understood broadly.) It should be noted that the subsequent history of the patronage of the institute illustrates that the Egyptian Campaigner's wishes were certainly fulfilled with the very early support of Wellington as the institute's first 'Vice Patron'.
5. 'Prospectus of the United Service Museum', May/June 1831, RUSI archive.
6. *Ibid.*
7. *Ibid.*
8. 'Circular on the Formation of The Naval and Military Museum', July 1831, RUSI archive.
9. Altham, *op. cit.*, p.3.
10. 'Report of the Committee of the Naval and Military Library and Museum', August 1831, pp. 20-23, RUSI archive.
11. 'Request of Committe', *Journal of the Royal United Service Institution* (hereafter *JRUSI*), I 1857, p.3.
12. S.P. Huntington, *The Soldier and the State* (1957), pp.217-218.
13. F.R. Klingender, *Art and the Industrial Revolution* (1972), pp.92-95.
14. This follows, very broadly, some of the factors suggested by D.S.L. Cardwell in *The Organisation of Science in England* (1957). Cardwell himself called the process the 'proliferation of societies and philosophical institutes' (p.27). The specific dates given about the formation of the Lit and Phil societies is taken from J. Morrell and A. Thackery, *Gentlemen of Science* (1981), p.12.
15. It must also be emphasised that this brief sketch of developments cannot do justice to the range and quality of some of the literature in this field. For example, the integration of these themes by J. Morrell and A. Thackery (1981), with the wider claim that the BAAS was also a political device 'for uniting elements of the better classes' at a time of the unrest surrounding the introduction of The First Reform Act of 1832 is immensely convincing. (pp. 11-12.) Likewise, so is the claim made by F.M. Turner that the later debate over the validity of Darwin's theory had rather more to do with the political control of university senates and professors chairs than epistemology versus theology. 'The Victorian Conflict Between Science and Religion: A

Professional Dimension', *Isis* 69 (1978), pp. 356-376.
16. C.A. Russell, *Science and Social Change 1700- 1900* (1983), p177.
17. *Ibid.*, p183.
18. A. Quinton, *Bacon* (1980), p.66.
19. C. A. Russell, *op. cit.*, p.191.
20. A. Quinton, *op. cit.*, p.67.
21. One could also argue that the Baconion emphasis on the limited role of the individual in science as a whole was also a description of a social order British officers could psychologically identify with. The subordination of the individual to a higher cause and the recognition of one's minor role in a larger enterprise would have come easily to officers trained to understand their role in battle in precisely the same terms.
22. Quoted in J. Morrell and A. Thackery, *op. cit.*, p.19.
23. I. Inkster and J. Morrell, *Science in British Culture, 1780-1850* (1983), p.94.
24. *Ibid.*, p.94.
25. This table is taken from Russell, *op. cit.*, pp. 194-195.
26. *Ibid.*, p.194.
27. *Ibid.*, p.197.
28. Chairman's Address, *JRUSI*, Vol. 1, 1857, p.1. It is interesting that Kew should also be picked out as a shining example of scientific success in the period from 1830. In fact, in *The Royal Botanic Gardens Kew* (1908), W. J. Bean argues that 'the twenty-one years between the death of George III and 1841 saw Kew at its lowest ebb,' (p.25.) It is therefore probable that Kew was picked out, not because of any great scientific success in this period, but because it had a long association with the Admiralty who had paid the expenses of Kew's foreign collectors for many years. See for example, Dr Lindley 'Copy of the Report made to the Committee appointed by the Lords of the Treasury in January 1838 to inquire into the management of the Royal Gardens', p.3. (Kew Botanical Gardens archive.).
29. 'Circular' 1831, *op.cit.*, pp 9-10, RUSI archive.
30. 'Sixth Annual Report of the Council', 1837, p.12. RUSI archive.
31. *Ibid.*, p.8.
32. Inkster and Morrell, *op. cit.*, p.99.
33. *Ibid.*, p.12.
34. *Ibid.*, p.9.

35. Altick called this the 'materialistic' attitude of the age.
36. Quoted in Inkster and Morrell, *op. cit.*, p.111.
37. J. Keegan, *The Mask of Command* (1987), p.139.
38. Keegan, *op. cit.*, pp. 92-155.
39. Klingender, *op. cit.*, p.93.
40. W. Vaughan, *Romantic Art* (1978), p.45.
41. Morrell and Thackery, *op. cit.*, p17.
42. Altham, *op cit.*, p.3. This moral ambition that the pursuit of science would divert officers from the club house, however, met with some resistance. In an answer to applications from members who had obviously not fully grasped this aspect of the institute's goals, a notice in 1836 said: '[T]he Council take this opportunity of stating, that in making their selection [of periodicals, etc.,] they adhere to their original resolution, excluding newspapers as unsuited to the professional and scientific character of the institution.' 'Fifth Annual Report of Council' 1836, p.183, RUSI archive.
43. 'Report of the Committee' 1831, p.10, RUSI archive.

CHAPTER THREE
SUCCESS FROM CRISIS: THE PUBLICATION OF THE INSTITUTION'S JOURNAL (1857-1861)

I

The publication of the first issue of the *Journal of the United Service Institution* in 1857 represents an important step in the development of the professional study of military science and military history in the British context. The early founders of the Institution had recognised that, finances permitting, it would be desirable for them to publish a journal of their proceedings. It gradually became apparent, however, that some sort of publication would become an absolute necessity if the original purposes of the Institution were to be brought anywhere near to fruition.

After 1839 the 'United Service Museum' was renamed 'The United Service Institution' (henceforth USI). This change of title reflected the domination of the council by the followers of Hardinge who continued the battle to achieve their ideal of the new professional officer. From this point on, however, a recurrent problem confronted this group. While the museum surpassed the founders' expectations, in terms of attracting members of the public to the Institution, it was clear that actual membership from the officer corps, although superficially high compared to other scientific bodies in London, was in fact stagnating (see Table overleaf).

This stagnation was due, in part, to the club house attitude of many serving officers that the Institution had always sought to combat. But it was also due to the key factor of British military service noticed by Best—the geographic dispersal of the Army. Since the scientific focus revolved around in-house activities, such as the seasonal public lecture, officers on the active service list could not attend these events regularly even if they had the inclination to do so. This meant that the Institution's push to involve more scientific officers was restricted to senior officers already in London, officers in partial or full retirement, and the relatively few junior officers attached to the regiments garrisoned in or around the London area. Clearly, such a relatively small active constituency was not going to create the sort of wider scientific army envisaged. The reality of British service life therefore threatened the continued existence of the USI as something more than a London museum. Indeed, these worries intensified over the next decade with the decreasing size of the officer corps. A report of 1842 observed that while the prosperity of the institute was for the moment assured, and while 127 officers had enrolled that year, 'this number, however, [fell] short of ... expectations'.[1]

Year	No. of Members	No. of Visitors
1831	1900	...
1832	3020	...
1833	3750	...
1834	3977	13 376
1835	4193	8537
1836	4087	8521
1837	4212	10 907
1838	4222	15 788
1839	4233	16 248
1840	4302	17 120
1841	4285	19 421
1842	4142	21 552
1843	4096	27 056
1844	4009	22 767
1845	4033	21 767
1846	4056	32 885
1847	4032	38 699

(Source: 'Proceedings of the Seventeenth Anniversary Meeting' (1848), p.8. RUSI archive.)

Success from Crisis

The initial response to the problem by the Council was to increase its overtures to the officers of both services. These overtures sought to publicise the scientific facilities available to members and to encourage their greater use. By 1840 this included new apparatus like a modern microscope. These yearly improvements in the equipment, and the employment of specialist staff to give instruction in their use, actually made little impact on the membership figures. It eventually became clear that the Institution could not break through this ceiling on its activity and that the council would have to widen the organisation's basis if it was to succeed. The literature of the period reflects this central problem. While there are many enthusiastic reaffirmations of its original goals, there is also a recognition that the year 1857 was to be a key moment in the Institution's history. A speech delivered by the Duke of Cambridge while the Crimean War was in progress in 1855 reflects the strong patronage the institute still enjoyed. The tone and content of his speech, however, which echoed comments made some twenty-five years earlier, illustrate that very little progress had been made.

> Some of the gentlemen who have spoken today have referred to the advantages of the Institution in a scientific point of view... I assure you I will endeavour personally to use any influence I may possess to impress upon the Government the advantages of this Institution in a scientific and educational point of view... The war has, however, evoked a military spirit in the country which we ought to take advantage of, and I firmly believe if we now strike while the iron is hot, we may succeed in getting a more general recognition of the advantages which the two branches of the Service derive from institutions of this description. There can be no doubt that science has advantages in every profession, but it is of more consequence in the military and naval professions than in any others. Even in a social point of view it is of the utmost advantage that military and naval men should be associated together, and should be afforded an opportunity of discussing together those improvements in the art of warfare which science and modern invention may have called into existence... So whether we regard this Institution in a social or in a scientific point of view, it is of equal importance to Her Majesty's Service. [2]

Although such firm support was welcomed, a simple reaffirmation of its goals and merits would not bring the wider army around to the Institution's point of view, nor alone, could it rekindle the early enthusiasm for the project. To meet the challenge and widen its appeal the USI undertook three new projects. Firstly, the new council of 1857 sought to move away from the earlier style in which a lecture was delivered at the institute by the leading figures of the London scientific circuit and Fellows of the Royal Society. This style reflected the fashion of attending lectures and experiments and had been adopted to give the new scientific body an immediate status. It had become apparent, however, that this approach was not what the wider army now needed or wanted. In order to heighten interest in the latest developments in professional matters, rather than simply to elucidate underlying cause and effect in natural phenomena, a new series of lectures would be delivered at the institute by leading military authorities. To achieve this goal, and obtain a pool of experts, the council sought to forge closer ties with the traditional 'scientific corps' within the Army, the artillery and the engineers. To this end, Col. Dixon of the Royal Artillery, Col. Wilford of Hythe (then a musket and artillery range) and Col. MacDougal of Sandhurst College were approached to give papers. As Col. James Lindsay, the new driving force behind these changes, saw it: 'We have among our members officers of the highest talent and ability, eminently capable of imparting the knowledge they have acquired, and of giving the service the benefit of their experience. The professional papers of the Royal Engineers are of the highest order, and amply prove what I say.'[3]

Secondly, it was proposed that the institute ought to do more to encourage the idea that it was a scientific board. Some members were somewhat upset that, prior to 1857, 'articles of a warlike character' were placed for exhibition at the 'Royal Society of Arts' rather than at the USI. This snub, they felt, reflected the fact that the institute was still not yet held by the Army, inventors or the general public in high esteem. This would be rectified, they argued, if the council provided the funds to facilitate exhibitions of their own.[4] This plan was carried through with models of small-scale engineering projects being brought

Success from Crisis

to the Institution by companies like Messers Russell and Cliffords. Contemporary large-scale engineering projects, such as the problem of laying the famous telegraph cable under the Atlantic, were also illustrated and discussed by officers interested in the question.

These two initiatives, however, were really only to be made meaningful with the launch of a journal of proceedings. In this publication, ultimately funded by the government, the council proposed to print abstracts of the new style lectures and the subsequent discussions that took place.[5] In issuing these proceedings three or four times a year and sending them to members serving in all parts of the world the Council hoped that they would now offer something to serving officers. Having failed to draw enough active members to the institute to radically change the wider army, the USI planned, as Lindsay put it, 'to go to them'.[6]

The pressure to change the direction of the USI was not simply the result of the stagnating membership figures and fading enthusiasm. External criticism of the early attempts by the Council to bring the scientific world and the military worlds together revolved around the feeling, articulated by both members and non-members in the services, that its activity was not felt to be strictly relevant to contemporary military demands. Consequently, the thinking behind the publication of a journal was that it could kill two birds with one stone. Not only would a journal draw more officers into thinking and being practically involved in professional matters, in line with the founders' original ambition, but the wider distribution of the knowledge produced would in turn give the institute a function and concrete role within the services as a whole. This role, it was hoped, would make the redefined Institution '*practically useful*, by promoting and encouraging information which must be beneficial' to the armed services.[7] On the eve of the publication of the first issue, there was a high level of optimism that this new role would succeed in 'not only [raising] the character of the Institution, but [morally] the character of those who compose it'.[8] In the key-note speech laying out this plan for the future, Lindsay sought to capture the balanced optimism of the moment:

In pursuance of the plan detailed, we propose to send an address to the officers of the several services, detailing our objectives and requesting their support... we may not be as successful as we would wish, yet the address will have the effect of impressing our designs upon the officers and make them acquainted with the merits and objects of the establishment... Upon the whole we have every reason to be sanguine for the future, and that we have passed the most difficult period of our career; and I trust it will be the pleasing duty of the future Chairman of the Council, in opening the lecture season, to congratulate you upon the *successful progress of professional science, as developed by the proceedings of this Institution. (emphasis added)* [9]

II

The contents of the early issues of the *Journal* reflect the key themes of military relevance and practicality and also start to develop the scientific concerns that the proceedings of the institute would address more fully in its maturity prior to 1914. For example, the lectures delivered, as promised, by Cols. Wilford and Dixon in the first year were both motivated by the desire to have the rifle replace the traditional musket as the British Army's standard infantry weapon. Virtually from its first issue, therefore, the *Journal* became the forum where supporters of a new technology sought to convince the wider army that these technological advances were destined to be part of 'modern warfare'. There was, however, something of a paradox in this early intellectual activity. When the British officers of this period used the term 'modern warfare', many were nevertheless thinking historically. 'Modern Warfare' meant, essentially at this specific point in the British development of the professional study of military affairs, what Wellington did up until 1815. Thus, in an 1857 paper by a Lt. Walker of the Royal Engineers, entitled 'On Military Tactics', the author articulated a developmental historical analysis that would not have seemed out of place to an officer in Wellington's army. After introducing the development of standing armies, Walker argued that 'the individual efficiency of the soldier, together with the art of moving masses of troops, improved gradually, until Frederick the Great brought the modern system of tactics to the highest state of efficiency'.[10] While the historical idea of 'modern warfare' was therefore on the agenda of the Institution's publication from the first year, the concern that rapid future technological change might radically undermine Wellington's version of the Enlightenment system of strategy, tactics and organisation was still not, in itself, a topic for consideration. Lt. Col. Dixon's first contribution to the new journal, 'The Rifle—Its Probable Influence on Modern Warfare' displays the intelligent British officer's attitude to this 'modern' concern.[11] In his introduction he points out that the problem for the soldier when considering technological advancements was to 'avoid forming possibly exaggerated notions of what may be anticipated from the ... soldier in future warfare.'[12] Splitting the higher levels of Enlightenment or British Wellingtonian strategy from the technological alterations to the standard infantry weapon, he argued:

> I have not considered it necessary to introduce strategy as likely to be directly affected by the introduction of the rifle, except in so far as a better armed and better instructed army, and one with its commissariat and whole interior economy better managed, than those of its adversary, may give greater confidence to the general commanding, in arranging the lines of operations, objective points, and in short the whole plan of campaign.[13]

This represents a very characteristic British military attitude of the time. An officer like Dixon could be, on the on one hand, passionate about the importance of the technological change he was advocating, while on the other, he could advocate that the correct general approach that any officer should take to technological change ought to be a sober conservative one. There was also a second methodological problem encountered by Dixon that would subsequently be confronted by each expert presenting papers at the USI. This difficulty relates to the 'gap' between the mere technical description and function of a weapon system and the description or prediction of its future effect on the course of any given expected battle or form of warfare. (For the British officer of this period, this battle was perceived to be the destruction of a French army landing somewhere between Portsmouth and Southend.) Dixon already alludes to the intractable nature of this problem. After giving what he takes to be a value-free discussion of the history and results of ballistic experiments of the competing rifles (Lancaster, Enfield, Armstrong, Whitworth) then being tested by the British Army, he says:

> I come to that part which touches upon the future of the arm, in relation to its probable influence on modern warfare... This subject is one which least of all will bear to be treated dogmatically. *I come to it with considerable diffidence*, and own that in the matter of mere opinion I am not more likely to form a correct, or as correct a one as many an officer who has also carefully studied the art of war. At the same time I do not shrink from drawing out discussion upon this interesting point. (*emphasis added*) [14]

The language that is used here, the caution that even the expert in the field displays, is central to the two faces of the study of military science the new institute sought to usher in. For, whatever the public claims of the Institution to be scientific may have been in 1857, for the officer actually engaged in predicting future warfare, it was already tacitly acknowledged that the ultimate seat of his claim to expertise rested, not on any over-arching scientific theory, but on his rank, reputation and experience. Consequently, when confronted with a dissenting voice of equal weight, no obvious recourse to overcome the impasse could easily be found. In short, while the redefined Institution sought to rest its claim to science on the professional authority of its expert membership, thinking members, characterised by Dixon, were already tacitly admitting that what they singularly did not have was the theoretical means with which to resolve the inevitable argument their advocacy raised. It is important to notice, however, that at this time, the *lessons* taught by recent historical examples were not specifically used by Dixon in his argument for the introduction of the rifle. In the context of the 1850s, those officers, like Walker, who had lectured on modern historical subjects, had also not demanded that it be given such a predictive role. Because 'modern war' was already seen as a perfected form of war, and officers such as Dixon did not expect vast changes to the British system even after the introduction of new technology like the rifle, in such circumstance predicting fundamental change would obviously have seemed a redundant activity.

Secondly, these very early discussions about technological progress, tactics and the role of military history have also to be understood against the backdrop of an earlier intellectual exchange that had already taken place in Prussia at the turn of the century. In the aftermath of Prussia's defeat at Jena in 1806, the German philosopher Johann Gottlieb Fichte (1762-1814) exhorted his countrymen to consider the wisdom of Machiavelli's military thinking. In an open letter, the then relatively unknown Clausewitz, while apologising to Fichte, sought to convince the philosopher that Machiavelli had really nothing to teach them in military affairs. 'So far as Machiavelli's book on the art of war itself is concerned', argued Clausewitz, 'I recall missing the free, independent judgement that so strongly distinguishes his political writing. The art of war of the ancients attracted him too much, not only in its spirit, but also in its form... Improvements today as always should never be sought by returning to an earlier pattern, but by restoring the true spirit of war, which will create its own appropriate forms and techniques.'[15]

Clausewitz was to return to this issue in *On War*, arguing that the 'further you go back the less useful military history became', and he added that 'the history of Antiquity is without doubt the most useless... We are in no position to apply it... to the wholly different means we use today.'[16] The implication of this, when understood strictly, is that the historical heuristic or methodology sanctioned by Clausewitz is that the officer seeking to understand modern war should consider only the most recent historical examples. Although not well-known at the mid century in England, Clausewitz, and the problem of what history to draw one's lessons from, would ultimately be a key debate among British military intellectuals.

Like their Prussian forebears, to some historically trained British officers of the 1850s and 60s it would not have seemed clear that such a rejection of Machiavelli and, *a fortiori*, the classical humanist tradition, would be at all warranted. In the British context, while there was not an objection to Wellington's version of the Enlightenment form of warfare being called 'modern warfare', to many minds an obsession with teaching military history only from this one period was seen as a dangerous thing. The early contributions of Col. MacDougal, for example, display a professional interest in the ancient world as well as Wellington. He lectured on aspects of the Punic Wars and recommended Caesar's *Commentaries* and the Chevalier Folard's *Polybius* for the young officer to study. A Rev. R Burgess compared the military roads of Rome with the emerging British railway system, and, in 'The Armies of Ancient Greece' the Rev. G. R. Glieg, the Chaplin-General, argued against the narrow historical education that the military cadet received in the 'army crammers'. These proponents of the continued relevance of classical education, and therefore of the value of ancient examples, were, however, as aware of their changing social and technological environment as the admirer of Wellington. Glieg, in the introduction to his paper, makes this perfectly clear:

> It can be no secret to any one here present that we are on the eve of great changes, and I hope of great improvements, in many points which bear upon the general arrangements of our army. I believe that before long the profession of arms will take its proper place in public estimation—that young men intended for the service will themselves see, and their relatives be taught, that they must exercise their minds as well as their bodies before they enter it; and that officers ... will be led to perceive that they have undertaken... [a] practice... which requires as much study as any other art or science with which common men are familiar.[17]

The professional ambition that lay behind Glieg's lecture, like the other supporters of wider historical study, was to convince his audience that the underlying principles of the 'art of war' were the same throughout history, and while tactics necessarily change with the 'progress of time and invention', higher aspects, such as strategy or good command, were universal. This attitude, methodologically, stands at the cross-roads of the 'Letters' between Fichte and Clausewitz. While Glieg does not follow Machiavelli's theoretical position in advocating a move, quite literally, back to an earlier form of warfare at a tactical or operational level, he certainly insists upon the classical world's continued relevance at the higher level. In the new forward looking environment of the 1860s, he felt that military education should encompass the wider historical heritage. 'War', Glieg reminded his audience, 'has been treated as an art, not by moderns only.'[18] Indeed, attacking, rather boldly, the narrow concern with the 'modern system' of war, he concluded that, 'there are other fountains whereat the military student may drink, with refreshment to himself, besides the despatches of the Duke of Wellington and the *Commentaries of Jomini* and of the Arch-Duke Charles.'[19]

III

The most profound work from this early period was most certainly by Capt. H.W.Tyler R.E. in 1860, 'The Rifle and the Spade, or the Future of Field Operations' (Sir Henry Whatley Tyler became a 2nd Lieutenant in 1844 and left the army in 1866. He became Chairman of the Westing House Brake Company and Deputy Chairman of the Great Eastern Railway Company. He died in 1908). This lecture is significant as it the first piece of work that seriously attempts to integrate the emerging technological and historical concerns of the new institute. Tyler, like Fuller, clearly had a fine military mind. In this paper the author senses that conditions on the battlefield would indeed change dramatically with the introduction of the modern rifle. Methodologically, Tyler, in his first paper for the USI, was still clearly Baconian in his view of his own necessarily limited role in the progress of military knowledge. This limited participatory role, within the context of the military community as a whole, is also put forward with the same diplomatic tact as Dixon had shown in his paper:

> [T]here is no question more interesting to military men, or more important to the world in general, at the present day, than that of the

effect which the modern rifle may be expected to produce... I make no apology for thus coming forward, although I do so with great deference to many amongst my audience who are much better qualified to speak upon the subject. I think it is of great importance, and it is the duty of military men, to discuss this question. *I believe that, by careful study and reflection, we may, looking from our own point of view, each add our mite to its better understanding.* (emphasis added) [20]

For Tyler, the title of his lecture was not meant to imply a parochial discussion of the spade as a common piece of civil and military equipment; rather he saw this tool as emblematic of the means by which the soldier could be covered from enemy fire and deal out, as he put it, his 'sixty rounds of ammunition'.[21] He rightly detected that the old solution to missile weapons—increasing the amount of protective armour worn—was no longer viable. What the soldier had to do now for protection was to 'contrive' field fortifications in the circumstances as they presented themselves on the battlefield. In his technical argument, he suggested that fairly effective field entrenchments could be constructed in as little as five hours while an almost impassable entrenchment could be built by six men in sixteen hours.[22] Importantly, Tyler did not wish to convince his audience that this interest in defensive measures was the *new lesson* or trend derived from the Crimean War; rather he attempts to convince his audience that his system of 'temporary parapets' was particularly suitable to the pre-existing British system of warfare. Entrenchments, he suggested, were 'particularly applicable to the defensive-offensive, or Wellingtonian system of operations, as it is termed, to which our great successes have been mainly due'.[23]

While Tyler was perfectly aware of the remarkable 'perseverance' of the Russian resistance against the combined might of Britain, France and Turkey in the Crimea, he does not use this example in the spirit of Clausewitz's methodological dictum. Rather, he seeks to convince that this new form of war is essentially what the British had, during the last century, always attempted to carry out in embryo form. Thus, Wellington's use of the 'reverse slope' and fortified use of the available farm houses at Waterloo was only an illustration of what, with a little foresight and organisation, might be conducted by a British army in future. There was, however, an important historical caveat to this question in his analysis. The practice of taking advantage of hedges, walls, banks, woods and trenches, he also argued, was 'better understood' in earlier times and this knowledge 'of late' has 'been too little appreciated'. [24] This remark illustrates that Tyler was also boldly rejecting the idea that the Wellingtonian system was not in need of some improvement. Even at Waterloo, he tells his audience, much loss of life would have been saved had there been more sappers, more tools, and infantry better instructed in the art of field engineering. Indeed, much like Machiavelli—and unlike Clausewitz—the implicit claim being made is that the modern system of war may have, in fact, degenerated from earlier forms.

Looking to bring his knowledge of antiquity to bear, Tyler finds his specific example for the conduct of a *future war* in the defensive field practice of the Roman Army: the 'Roman legionaires', he argued, 'were employed to fortify their camps with a rampart some twelve feet high and twelve feet or more wide ... Works of a similar magnitude will be required for the protection of future armies.'[25] Advocates of the utility of ancient military history would have no doubt applauded this argument even if Tyler did not seem too worried about deeper underlying principles. Indeed, Tyler's subtle appeal to the improvement of the Wellingtonian tradition by means of an ancient example was instantly recognised as an important contribution to modern military thinking. In response to his claim that the emblem of modern warfare ought to be the spade, Sir John Burgoyne (1782-1871), one of the leading soldiers of his day, praised whole-heartedly Tyler's paper for being 'early in the field of research' and for submitting 'many valuable observations as a commencement'. Adding that the members of the Institution ought to be ready to consider 'much alteration in the system of warfare... after much studied consideration given to the subject, and much practice, and even experience in actual war'.[26]

This early belief by officers such as Tyler and Burgoyne that the future form of warfare was to be shaped by rifles and trenches, already has an important bearing on the claims made later by Liddell Hart and Fuller. Clearly, the problems posed by these contemporary technological advances were on the USI's redefined agenda from as early as 1857. From the literature it is also perfectly clear that the demand that there should be an environment in which the effects of these advances could be discussed was also being made by many thinking British officers at this time. More importantly, what papers like Tyler's illustrate is that there were, by any fair standard, 'extraordinary' and perceptive minds at the centre of, and writing at, the very moment the British military intellectual 'seat of authority' was being established in the mid-century. Ironically, the particular tool of labelling and lampooning one's opponents as 'ultra-conservative', often used with great effect by Fuller and Liddell Hart in their later campaign, was also first articulated by the forward thinking Tyler. In his next paper, called 'The Rifle and the Rampart, or the Future of Defence', he tackled this very real, and in the context of the British Army of 1860, very considerable grouping of conservatives he faced:

> There are still a number of nice, dear, old ladies in this country—long may they live in it—who consider steam engines and railways as nasty, dangerous things, who believe that people have no right to be whirled through the air at the awful speeds of the present day, and who are firmly resolved not to place their valuable lives, at all events, at the disposal of any board of railway directors. It would answer no good end, of course, to talk to these otherwise sensible persons, of the enormous results which these 'new fangled machinations' have already produced, any more than of those which they are destined to bring about, in the different relations of mankind. In like manner, there are many distinguished members of the sterner sex, younger in years, and military by profession, who look through a veil of prejudice at the improvements which are taking place in the weapons of war. They cannot but consider rifled muskets and guns, and elongated projectiles, to be nasty dangerous things; but they are convinced, nevertheless, that they will not produce, after all, much alteration in the actual practice of war. They regret to see such weapons being introduced into the ser-

vice. They fear that the relations which had previously existed, and which ought in their opinion still to be maintained between the three main arms are in danger of being disturbed... It would be an equally thankless task to discuss with them the possible effects of these improvements, and still more so to dwell with them upon those interesting reflections, as to the power which the possession of such means of destruction confers upon civilisation, and upon the helpless condition in which barbarism will, in the end, be relatively placed.[27]

IV

While leading military intellectuals of the period, like Tyler, started to work through the problem of what the future might bring, and how one even began to discuss these questions, there were still those within the Army who also wished to discuss the wider questions of science and technology. Maj. Gen. Portlock, an old friend of Hardinge, and member of the 'Council of Military Education', gave a paper in 1859 called 'On the Advantage of Cultivating the Natural and Experimental Sciences, as Promoting the Social Comfort and Practical Utility of Military Men'. This lecture is of specific interest as it is one of the last serious attempts to revive the Lit and Phil inspired ideal of the officer as a natural scientist held by the early members of the institute. In his central argument Portlock, also a Baconian, while not rejecting the value of the study of the classics and pure mathematics in an education for professions such as the law or the church, argued that the natural sciences provided a better and particularly suitable education for the army officer. He explained that the natural sciences exercised 'the highest faculties of the mind' and had great merit for the officer that they also tempted 'the student to the fields or to the mountains, promoting the health of the body whilst invigorating the mind'.[28] Portlock advocated the value of this type of education in the same moral terms articulated some thirty years before. The 'natural sciences', he said, 'promote and increase the happiness of a man by setting him above any little difficulties or disagreeable circumstances which may surround him'.[29] From the specific illustrations he used in his text it is clear that he was also particularly excited by the relevance

51

of Charles Lyell's (1779-1875) *Principles of Geology* (1830-1833) to the practical problems faced by the officer in the field.[30] Quoting his friend Sir Joseph Hooker (1817-1911) with obvious approval, Portlock related to his audience this eminent botanist's view of the British military's contribution to science.

> Dr Hooker ... says, and I am convinced it is a perfectly just observation, though some perhaps at the present day may not be disposed to admit it, 'It is a curious fact that the majority of those military and naval men who have been distinguished for their love of natural history have also been renowned in their profession: witness Cook, King, Parry, Ross, Richardson, Franklin, in the navy; and you can no doubt match these names in the army, by such as Eyre, General Hardwick, and Champion, a capital botanist... shot at Inkerman.'[31]

The central problem for the remaining proponents of the officer as scientist was, however, the progress in the 'experimental sciences' as they related directly to electrical and mechanical engineering. Portlock argued that progress in these fields was leaving even the most capable of the military naturalists behind. After a discussion of the latest developments in electro-magnetic technology, he alluded to what he described as a widespread feeling among many British officers 'that they [were] unable to compete in scientific matters with such men as [Prof.] Wheatstone' (Sir Charles Wheatstone 1802-1875, produced the first practical electric telegraph in 1837).[32] The failure of soldiers to take the lead in this branch of scientific knowledge was critical, he felt, given the emerging importance of engineering and telegraphy in military affairs. Portlock argued that this situation could be rectified by the adoption of the form of scientific education for officers he was advocating. This goal, of having soldiers themselves actually leading investigations into the applications of electro-magnetic discoveries, now seems a little over-optimistic. The fact that leading figures in the British Army, like Portlock, should have been concerned that the military should have direct involvement—or even control—over these fields of enquiry demonstrates that the rapid pace of progress in the mechanical sciences had become the central concern for the traditional supporters of a scientific military education. Portlock's advocacy of scientific education for young officers, however, was still framed in terms of the same demand for improved military efficiency that had appealed to the supporters of the USM a generation before. 'It [a scientific education]', he argued, 'is an advantage to all military men, particularly those in the corps of Artillery and Engineers, to possess a description of knowledge which awakens their facilities, and excites them to overcome difficulties, to avoid bungling arrangements, and to introduce improvements.'[33]

This is where he departed significantly from the values of the new Institution. Given the narrow professional interest of the new Council, and the articulation of these interests by Tyler and Burgoyne, it would have probably surprised leaders of the Council, like Lindsey, to hear that the officers of the corps of Artillery and Engineers were in particular need of a new scientific education. The redefinition of the professional goals of the Institution were predicated on the assumption that these corps already had a high level of professional scientific competence. Rather than produce the science or technology itself, the new role for the scientific officers of these corps was to understand its future use. Indeed, when one considers the internal debate and the new structure of the USI immediately before and after 1858-59, we find that the sort of scientific involvement for the Institution re-articulated by Portlock had, in fact, already been deemed a failure by the wider army and by key leaders of the USI. Military science, as mediated through the Institution, was to become an attempt by an intellectual elite, to guide, through rational debate and the proceedings of its *Journal*, the future course of the Army. While the council of the institute could clearly tolerate the publication of Portlock's article in the *Journal*, his ambition for British soldiers to lead the field in the various branches of mechnical science was already pretty dated when it was published. It certainly no longer reflected what the institute would be actively seeking to carry out as its own scientific mission in the context of the British military as a whole. Indeed, the first target for the supporters of the new, more narrowly defined, role for the institute had already fallen. Taking, as one member put it, a 'pruning knife' to the natural history collection it was decided that the institute could no longer vie with those other scientific institutions in London that made the subject their speciality and that the other departments too would have to be made subservient to the new ends of the institute.[34] As chairman of the council in 1858, Lindsey had already put forward the simple choices to be made:

> Now, gentlemen, there is this point to be borne in mind. If you are inclined to become no more than a museum, nothing is so easy as to do it. You may reduce half your expenditure at once, and having done so you may say, take a shilling at the doors, people will be glad to see the museum. But if you have higher motives, if you have higher aspirations, you have the means to carry them into effect yourselves. It is only to be done by the active cooperation of all the members who are serving on full pay. Now I know there is a great difficulty there; the great bulk of officers are serving abroad... and therefore they naturally say, 'Of what use is this institution to us?' It has been perfectly true. I do not deny it. Our object now is to make the Institution valuable to all: and if we can carry that object into effect by means of the *Journal*, the numbers of which are now lying upon the table, we hope to carry the Institution to those officers. There is more than ten shilling's worth of information in that book—it is worth the money—and we hope by means of that book to carry the Institution to them, and to get them to come to us, in spirit in any rate, if they cannot do so in person.[35]

The proof of the validity of Lindsey's resolve and the success of the *Journal* among the British officer corps was soon felt. The membership figures for 1858-59 showed that the numbers who joined that year exceeded the numbers who joined (bar one) in any year since 1837. Not only did 222 new members join but the leaders of the institute pointed out that these officers joined 'without the slightest exertion' from the Institution. Given the struggle that had been experienced in the past in attracting new members, Lindsey thought this must reflect 'the improvements and the progress' which they had made.[36] Indeed, so confident was the Council that the Institution had finally carved out a lasting new scientific role for itself in the structure of the British military, that they took the opportunity in 1859 to offer their new *Journal* in exchange for the military journals of the other major foreign military powers.[37]

In the next section the problems of institutional arrangements and long-term goals, which as the discussion above suggests were all but resolved at this point, gives way to a discussion of the detailed historical, historiographical, and technolgical problems officers faced in deciding what the future of warfare entailed both for the military profession and the British people.[38]

Notes

1. 'Proceedings at the Eleventh Anniversary Meeting', p.1. RUSI archive.
2. B. Burgess, 'A Brief History of The Royal United Service Institution' (1887), p.13. RUSI archive.
3. 'Chairman's Address' 1857, *op. cit.*, pp. 4-5.
4. *Ibid.*, p.5.
5. Altham, *op. cit.*, p.9. A £400 per annum grant was obtained through 'the good offices of Lord Panmure' (plus Tax relief on this amount).
6. Lindsay called this a '*quid pro quo*': 'Chairman's Address' (1857), *op. cit.*, p.5.
7. *Ibid.*
8. *Ibid.*
9. *Ibid.*
10. D.C. Walker, 'On Military Tactics', *Journal of the United Services Institute (JUSI)*, I (1857) p.256.
11. W.H.M. Dixon, 'The Rifle—Its Probable Influence on Modern Warfare', *JUSI*, I (1857), p.95.
12. *Ibid.*
13. *Ibid.*, p.109.
14. *Ibid.*, p.108.
15. Quoted in P. Paret, *Clausewitz and the State* (1976), p.176.
16. Quoted in A. Gat, *op. cit.* (1989), p.7.
17. R. Glieg, 'The Armies of Ancient Greece', *JUSI*, I (1857), p.30.
18. *Ibid.*, p.50.

19. *Ibid.*, p.50-51.
20. H.W. Tyler, 'The Rifle and the Spade, or the Future of Field Operations', *JUSI*, III (1860), p.170.
21. *Ibid.*, p.179.
22. *Ibid.*, p. 180.
23. *Ibid.*, p.182.
24. *Ibid.*
25. *Ibid.*, pp. 184-185.
26. *Ibid.*, Burgoyne in Chairman's address to meeting, p.194.
27. H.W.Tyler, 'The Rifle and the Rampart, or the Future of Defence', *JRUSI*, IV (1861), p.331. It is interesting to speculate if Liddell Hart had read this paper in the 1920s given the title of his own book, *Paris or the Future of War*.
28. Portlock, 'On the Advantages of Cultivating the Natural and Experimental Sciences, as Promoting the Social Comfort and Practical Utility of Military Men', *JUSI*, III (1859), p.294.
29. *Ibid.*, p. 294.
30. *Ibid.*, p. 294. Portlock also reminded his audience, in deeply Baconian terms, that the 'Book of nature is indeed inexhaustible, and wearies the less the more it was studied'.
31. *Ibid.*, p. 299.
32. Prof. Sir Charles Wheatstone was a pioneer of electric telegraphy in England. See, for example, L.T.C. Rolt, *Victorian Engineering* (1970).
33. Portlock, *op. cit.*, p.300.
34. 'Proceedings of the Twenty-Seventh Anniversary meeting' 1858, p.299. RUSI archive.
35. *Ibid.*, p.307
36. 'Chairman's Address' 1860, pp. 88-89. RUSI archive
37. *Ibid.*, 'We also thought it a good opportunity of entering into communication with foreign countries, and accordingly wrote letters to the representatives of foreign countries residing in this country, offering to transmit our *Journal* to their respective war departments, in the hope that they would transmit their naval and military magazines or reviews to our Institution. I may point to this table as the happy result of that request for the interchange of publications. The Prussian government have sent us twenty-two volumes of a military journal; the Russian government have sent us three of a military review.' The Institute also received journals from the Canton of Berne,

Sardinia and Denmark, p.89.

38. Quoted in, B.Burgess, *op. cit*, Appendix D, p.34. It should also be noted that the rapid consolidation of the new institute's position within the British military structure received the final seal of approval with both the support of the Under Secretary of State for War, Earl De Grey and Ripon, who publicly declared that he had 'the very highest appreciation of the value of the services rendered by [the] institution', and the granting and purchase of its Royal Charter of Incorporation in 1860.

CHAPTER FOUR
FIRST PERCEPTIONS OF THE AMERICAN CIVIL WAR: THE STRUCTURE OF VICTORIAN MILITARY THOUGHT (1861-1869)

[T]he tactical lessons of the Civil War were rejected by most European soldiers and recognised by only a few. In every instance when the experience of the American armies conflicted with popular opinion at home or the lessons of more recent wars, the latter prevailed. Most of those who studied the Civil War after 1870 were in reality seeking to confirm accepted principles rather than discover new information that lead to a change in doctrine. For this reason the tactical lessons of the Civil War went unheeded, proving again the wisdom of Bronsart von Schellendorf's observation: 'It is well known that military history, when superficially studied, will furnish arguments in support of any theory or opinion.'
J.Luvaas, *The Military Legacy of The American Civil War: The European Inheritance* (1988), pp.232-233.

I

As Burgoyne had stated after his discussion of Tyler's excellent work, to get a really firm grasp on future trends in warfare would not only require a willingness by the British to consider 'much alteration in the system of war' but also, in all likelihood, some real demonstration of the effects of railways, telegraphy and rifled ordnance. The American Civil War (1861-1865) started only five years after this practical requirement went onto the agenda of the institute. In an article called 'An English View of the Civil War', Viscount Wolseley (1833-1913) explained that the battles of the conflict had been watched with 'breathless interest and excitement... from month to month, almost from day to day' by the British.[1] Officers also went to North America to witness the preparations and the ensuing battles at first hand. Among their number included Maj. Gen. Sir George Bell, Lt. Col. Henry Charles Fletcher, Lord Hartington, Lt. Col. James Arthur Fremantle, and, as official military observers, Capt. T. Mahon, Capt. R. Grant and Lt. T.C. Price. The events they witnessed and the reports of the effects of the modern weapons used gradually filtered back to the British Army over the next few decades with the publication of their personal recollections and official reports about the war. Before this Civil War literature had been widely seen, the officers invited to lecture at the by now Royal United Service Institution (following the granting of a Royal Charter in 1860) attempted to formulate judgements on the conflict as it unfolded.[2]

The first major discussion of the war took place in 1862 and was given by Maj. F. Miller R.A. in a lecture entitled 'A Military Sketch of the Present War in America'. Like Wolseley, Miller recognised the widespread professional interest in the war. However, the first task he undertook at the RUSI was to warn fellow officers about the problems inherent in the popular literature they were receiving. 'The interest which we naturally feel in the American war' he said 'has been fed from day to day by the special correspondence of the leading journals, and the ordinary intelligence of the daily or weekly papers.'[3] 'Those notices, valuable as they are for the preparation of regular narratives', he felt, 'are apt to confuse as much as they inform us, unless we have the opportunity to treat them as study.'[4] Such a study he argued, should not only act as a corrective to the failings of journalists but also address the key questions of technological change as they related to the underlying principles of modern war. Lay-men were never to be wholly trusted by the members of the Institution. Alluding to its greater ambitions, he added:

> I need hardly say that a lecture delivered in this room should be something more than a mere summary of facts. If it treats of military history, it should point out how far principles were vindicated by the results

of observing or neglecting established rules, and how any new weapon or any new feature in the equipment of an army influenced its movement or affected its achievements.[5]

After a long and detailed discussion on the early campaigns of the war, up to the Battle of Bull Run, Miller observed that the Federalists had, with their immense manufacturing resources and extensive commerce, from 'the outset everything that a nation could want for the purposes of war, except an army'.[6] The main conclusion he reached, however, was not strictly in accord with his own stated methodological interest in technology. The contemporary debate over the status of the volunteer forces in England was clearly uppermost in his mind. Federal officers and men, he argued, were generally poor in battle. Indeed, if such untrained men and inexperienced officers 'snatched from civil pursuits' had been able rapidly to crush the South, the whole world, he thought, 'would have been amazed'. Implicitly defending the qualities of the British long-service system, he added rather philosophically that the professional soldier's life would, indeed, be wasted, and his occupation might well be gone, if thousands of men thus hurriedly called under arms could be marched and manoeuvred at will. That they could be thus handled no disinterested person was sanguine enough to suppose.'[7]

A second lecture entitled, 'The Recent Campaigns in Virginia and Maryland', given the following year, by Capt. C.C. Chesney RE, then professor of military history at Sandhurst, picked up on the key themes presented by Miller. While agreeing about the disasters of the first year of the war, Chesney argued that the Union army had greatly improved the following year. As a firm supporter of the volunteers in England, this later improvement by the Federal troops gave Chesney 'heartening assurance... that the volunteer system was not itself a vice'.[8]

Although he clearly wanted to use events to support this particular contemporary political cause, he also wished to address in his contribution the deeper question of the underlying principles of war. The campaigns represented, for Chesney, the ideal chance to test the modern system of warfare. While he would not be drawn on the thorny debate over 'how much soldiering could be learned by the mere study of books', if one wanted to profit from military history, then, for Chesney, these principles had to be addressed by the military student.[9] They were not too difficult to grasp as they exhibited the matters of geography and supply orientated features that had always been part of the art of generalship. Like the earlier writers, Chesney split the higher levels of strategy from tactical considerations. The guiding principles of strategy used by the American generals, he argued, 'animated Caesar, Hannibal and Napoleon', and at 'no time, save in exceptional cases, could generals deviate from those principles without meeting evil consequences'.[10] Indeed, his specific formulation of the rationale of contemporary military planning would have been instantly recognised by any of the earlier Enlightenment writers on the science of war:

> [A] modern army of any size cannot possibly enter into an enemy's country without taking with it large supplies, and also without having those supplies constantly replenished from some great depot *called a base*, which it leaves behind, and that, in consequence of that necessity, the general commanding is obliged to have *a line of communication* always open—never interrupted by the enemy—between himself and that base. The fact, again, that though two or three small armies cannot be expected long to resist two or three large armies... if [they] combine together, they might successfully attack and beat each of the other and larger armies [*defeat in detail*]. These three main facts—all simple enough when explained in themselves—give rise to certain rules; and, according to those rules, in some measure, campaigns must be weighed and tried. (*emphasis added*) [11]

This summary probably offers a taste of the form of military science taught by Chesney at this time at Sandhurst. He felt that this simple formulation was often presented in such 'very high and dry terms, that some officers make the world believe that they are impossible to be understood', or the principles were simply ignored by those who refused to study anything at all. Putting aside these two extremes, the key point of the Virginia campaign, he concluded, was the fact that it demonstrated the continued validity of these 'rules flowing from the facts' of even this modern war.[12]

II

Miller's statement of intent demonstrates that technological change was on the agenda of the RUSI even as it first looked at the war in North America. However, it was deemed by leading intellectuals to be of secondary importance to the study of military history and the demonstration of the continuing validity of the underlying principles. While these officers set out methodological promises that they would show an interest in technological novelties, their studies do not really address the issue. Repeating the earlier approach of Dixon, both Miller and Chesney implicitly assumed that technological change would lead only to modern European powers deciding a conflict somewhat more quickly and more efficiently than Wellington or Napoleon had managed to do. Secondly, it also needs to be recognised that the phrase 'learning the lessons' is not directly used by Miller or Chesney at this time.

Clearly, Chesney was interested in teaching, and by trivial definition he hoped his pupils would learn something. However, the specific use of the phrase, as articulated by modern British students of military history had not yet crystallised. A distinction between (1) the traditional activity of learning to avoid mistakes by understanding sound universal principles, and (2) learning lessons to make rational predictions about future trends in warfare is still absent in these very early discussions at the Institution about the American Civil War. This situation changed when the next lecture on the American conflict called 'Railways Strategically Considered', chaired by the Institution's new vice-patron, the Prince of Wales, was delivered by Tyler in 1864.[13] The first notable feature of this paper is that it represented the full development by him of the ideas found in 'The Rifle and the Spade' and 'The Rifle and the Rampart'. To make the introduction of his latest thoughts on changing modern warfare more acceptable to his peer group, Tyler predicated his discussion on the same underlying principles or 'facts' that Miller and Chesney had recommended. Attributing the assertion that 'legs were of more value than arms in war' to the Enlightenment theorist De Saxe, he suggested that the 'whole secret of war' consisted in marching.[14] 'Archduke Charles proves the truth of it... by showing that certain battles are won by successful strategy before they are fought.'[15] This seems to represent, for Tyler at least, a new found interest in the corpus of Enlightenment theories of war; echoing Chesney's earlier summary of its underlying principles he formulated his own version of its key features.

> [S]trategy is simply the art of moving military forces to the best advantage on a theatre of war; and the objects to be attained in the practice of it during a campaign (as well as in the practice of tactics in battle) are (1) to be superior at the proper time and at *the decisive point*, and (2) to threaten the *communications* of the enemy without exposing your own. Setting political considerations aside, war is from beginning to end a question of communications. (*emphasis added*) [16]

Attempting to intermix the legacy of the Roman military road building with this rationale of military operations that emphasised the role of manoeuvre, he suggested that, in drawing up a plan of campaign, the main consideration faced by a general was the routes along which the armies must pass. 'During a battle', he now argued, 'the victor looks mainly to the communications of his enemy.'[17] Nevertheless, this reaffirmation of the centrality of the lines of communication was really only a starting point for Tyler. He was not studying railways simply to confirm the validity of the Enlightenment principles then so cherished by the likes of Chesney. Wishing to gain prior agreement on the central undertaking of his thesis, he argued that if success in warfare rested on communications then it was a matter, he thought, 'of the highest interest to all military students to study the effect of railways upon the various operations of war' and to 'profit, as far as possible, by the experience which has been afforded in other countries'.[18] After an introduction that demonstrated he had a very sound knowledge of the first thirty-nine years of passenger railways in Great Britain, and how that system might well deliver 4000 to 5000 men at any point on the

South Coast, he argued that soldiers must re-adjust themselves to the new time scale introduced into warfare. Movement on roads, rivers and railways were all to be reduced to a common relative measure of time. In the military operations of the future, argued Tyler, 'victory is a question of days, or hours, or sometimes even minutes, in the movement of troops, when the forces are on anything like an equality'.[19]

Tyler's discussion, in terms of the specific historical content, offered a detailed account of the Italian Campaign of 1859 before moving onto the American Civil War, though the Italian campaign had only lasted two months and the American Civil War had, at the time of writing, dragged on for three years.[20] The main geographical feature of interest in the North American conflict was the sheer size of the theatre of operations. Because of the vast distances involved, and the poor quality of most of the roads, the railway network and the river system (along with the telegraph) were of 'paramount importance' from the military perspective. Tyler argued that the railway system had been the principal ally of the South. The railways, he suggested 'form the key by which almost all their inland operations may be understood; and their course has served to determine the site of almost all their positions'.[21] The North, on the other hand, had been tied to the lines of the rivers. No 'great Northern army', he observed, had 'been able to maintain itself for any length of time, even with the aid of railways, more than a days march from the sea or a great river.'[22]

As Jay Luvaas rightly claims, Tyler was not alone in observing that communications had become important. However, the subject warrants far more attention than it gets in *The Military Legacy of the Civil War*.[23] Instead of resting content with showing to brother officers that the underlying principles of warfare were still valid (which, incidentally, he did seem to believe) Tyler took it as his task to make some warranted predictions about the future aspects of the technology and its role in warfare. In attempting to do this he formulated a series of seven theses. Their content is no longer significant itself, but the theses are significant as the first example of the modern language of a predictive military science and, specifically, of the ideal of the learning of military lessons being used in the context of the RUSI.

> *The general lessons which may, it appears to me, be deduced from what is at present known on the subject,* are that: (1) Railways may, when available, be often used with great advantage on a theatre of war as an auxiliary means of moving troops, and as a principal means of supplying them. (2) Railways are more quickly and easily destroyed and more readily repaired (in a temporary manner) ... than common roads. (3) A single line of railway, in good order, and furnished with a proper proportion of sidings ... is sufficient for the ordinary supply of an army in the field ... (6) Railways may be employed to much greater advantage in defensive than in offensive operations. (7) Railway junctions will often become strategical positions of the greatest importance.[24]

As railways became more and more important, Tyler felt it would become necessary for every soldier in an army to be both able to repair and destroy them. Seamlessly drawing his latest piece of work into the context of his overall contribution to military thinking, Tyler felt that a radically re-organised army would be most 'desirable' in the new steam age.

> I have had occasion to point out in previous lectures that the use of the spade in warfare will necessarily increase with the common employment of, and with the growing proficiency in the use of rifled weapons; and I would now add that the use of railways in war will render it still more desirable that every soldier should be trained to be more or less of an engineer.[25]

When this seemingly modest argument is seen in context, 1864, in retrospect, becomes a very important year in the development of military thought in Britain. As suggested in the introduction, it was Fuller's assertion that very few officers in Europe prior to 1914 had seen or understood the *dominant tactical problem* that faced them. Fuller argued that it had been seen by him at the Camberley Staff College that year.[26]   Instead of looking backwards at principles of Napoloenic warfare, he asserted, British officers should have looked forward and predicted the effects of technology and scientific invention. Thus, 'tactics should be moulded around... the dominant weapons', the products of scientific invention.[27] However, it can clearly be seen that this general philosophical view preceded Fuller. Tyler, while paying all due respect to the established principles at the strategic level, specifically formulates predictions or lessons on emerging technological systems, in this case, the rifle, the spade and the railway. In this sense, Tyler had developed, in Fuller's terms, a scientific perspective of warfare (technology - weapon system - tactics - strategy), exactly forty-five years before the idea would be re-articulated by the interwar theorists.

Rather than reviewing the period as far removed from technological and scientific progress, it is clear that the language and the interest in learning lessons for future use was not retarded in the British context prior to 1870 but actually invented at this time. If one believed that war was fundamentally unchanging then there really was no need for such an interest in the future or the development of a language and science that attempted to make sense of it. The debate conducted at the RUSI illustrates that such an activity was clearly felt to be necessary. The decade of the 1860s can therefore rightly be seen as the first period in modern British military thought when soldiers really started to move from a vision of an essentially unchanging static system of war to contemplating and predicting its future. The historian Robert Altick suggests in *Victorian People and Ideas* (1973) that, 'Perhaps it might be said that the Victorians lived their everyday lives according to two times, the old leisurely one and the new headlong one'.[28] Their soldiers' early attempts at understanding the future of warfare therefore display not stupidity, or particular ignorance, but only military minds accustomed to the former sense of time genuinely grasping at the latter.

Tyler was not alone in focusing on the products of new technology and attempting to build on this base. Indeed, one of the features of his work about the future was that it also represented another Victorian attitude to emerging science and technology.[29] The idea that rapid change was part of an inevitable developmental process had already entered army circles from early supporters of Darwinian evolutionary biology. Following a series of three lectures on primitive warfare delivered by the now famous anthropologist, Col. A. H. Lane-Fox, at the institute in 1868, the splendidly named Capt. Vivian-Dering Majendie R.A., then 'Assistant Superintendent at The Royal Laboratory Woolwich' argued in distinctly evolutionary terms that 'the revival of breech loaders came exactly at the proper time, and as a sort of natural step or consequence in the development of firearms'.[30] Other early writers on military technology sought to develop a moral prescription from the rapid historical changes they were witnessing in the field of warfare. For example, in 1863 G.R. Burnell wrote in 'On the Recent Progress of the Military Sciences' that the alterations made to the art of defence and attack had made it 'necessary for the student to watch carefully the directions in which the *intellect of the age is turning*'.[31] The progress of guns, he felt, 'only leads to a corresponding advance in the art of defence against them, and both of these tendencies display themselves in the increase of the cost of the art of war, *which, it is to be hoped, will soon become so great as to render the recourse to it less frequent than it has hitherto been*'.[32] The moral thrust of this remark, of course, was that the technological change they were anticipating would, for military and economic reasons, lead to a better future in which there would be fewer wars fought.

This hope was also to be found discussed, surprisingly, in the first lecture on the machine gun delivered by Maj. G.V. Fosbery at the Institution in 1869. In a lecture entitled 'On Mitrailleurs, and Their Place in the Wars of the Future', Fosbery, like Tyler, was highly critical of soldiers (and laymen) who wished to bury their heads in the sand. Arguing against those who sought to limit the horrors of war by limiting the type of weapons involved to only those used in the past, he claimed that 'It has been so often, and so convincingly stated, that the loss of life in each fresh contest stands in an inverse rather than a direct ratio to the perfection of the arms made use of, and so evident a good to all engaged results from any limitation of the duration of war itself'.[33] This military use of an inverse-square law was apparently so well known that Fosbery did not credit its discoverer nor did he give any recent empirical data to support it. However, he did make quite clear his feelings for those who, out of a misplaced charity, would attempt to deny it. From his own perspective, while not necessarily claiming that there would be fewer conflicts, the great moral benefit of this particular square law suggested that what wars there were would be shorter.

> I shall not commence this paper by any apology for such attention as I have paid to a class of weapons which are called infernal or inhuman, only by superficial reasoners, or by those who fail to *comprehend the lessons conveyed by military statistics*. The arguments which condemn a warlike instrument simply on the grounds of its destructiveness to life... are, if logically pursued, simply retrogressive, and even if not recommending by implication a return to the bow and arrow, at all events point to the old times of protracted wars, and deaths from fatigue and disease, far exceeding in number those caused by the weapons of the enemy. We can... neglect them altogether, and seriously consider any invention which... promise us a more certainly destructive fire than that attainable, *caeteris paribus*, by the arms at present included in our material.[34]

After a technical discussion of the various types of machine gun then on test at Woolwich, and an illustration of the statistical results of the ballistics, Fosbery argued that the initial high cost of each gun would be far out-weighed by the savings made by the Army on the cost of 'highly trained and highly paid artillerymen' and the saving to be made on horse teams.[35] While this illustrates, perhaps, a little political naiveté on his part (and explains the Victorian Artillery corps' well-known dislike of the weapon) the key conclusion he wished to draw for his audience related to the larger picture of future warfare. Quoting from a 'clever pamphlet' on the supposedly secret mitrailleur by an anonymous French engineer, Fosbery explained that this author felt that military 'power was no longer on the side of the big battalions'.[36] Alluding to a special benefit that technology would give, this French author had added that, just as 'machinery has rendered industry rich and prosperous, so now whilst diminishing, or at least without increasing a war expenditure, it is about to render small peoples and little states as powerful for defence as are the great for attack'.[37] Fosbery could not agree entirely with this claim. He felt that to argue that the machine gun was purely a defensive weapon limited its considerable offensive value. All the same, he recognised that the French engineer had seen the central issue raised by the weapon, which was, as Fosbery put it, 'the multiplication of fire by mechanical means, and the saving of life and money so effected'.[38]

In conclusion, rather than being removed from modern concerns, it is in fact the case that the period up to 1869 saw the integration of the two central components of the structure of military science as it would be articulated by British officers prior to the Great War. The first achievement was the use of the language to refer to military lesson learning in the modern form. However, it must be observed that this approach to learning the lessons for future warfare from specific historical examples did not stand alone. It was made in the context of a larger set of values of a scientific and technological world view. This Victorian system of belief was morally charged and profoundly directed towards the future. As the examples above illustrate, warfare was recognised to be changing. It also seemed to be deductively the case, for the soldiers who accepted this premise, that the benefits science and technology had brought to industry would be brought to the conduct of war. Despite the obvious example of the American conflict, it was thought that a war fought by advanced European powers would, on the basis of the principles inherent in the new scientific system, be quick, cheap in economic costs and spare many human lives. In short, technological change would lead to the perfected ideal form of warfare as imagined by the advanced Victorian military mind.

Again, we must not judge from the perspective after 1918. In holding what now seems a profoundly mistaken view of what we call *industrial warfare*, these thinkers were not simply being blind to the obvious facts before them. While they did have to invent, at the time of the American conflict, a series of *ad-hoc* explanations to account for counter-examples, they were, even in their selection of over-arching metaphysical principles, in the vanguard of mid-Victorian philosophical thinking about progress, science and technology. As Altick says, it was widely held that 'time' and 'change' were related and that society was by necessity moving in some direction. This belief, he notes, 'was not a matter of faith but of common observation... To the typical Victorian mind, sanguine in temperament and materialistic in its values, the answer [to this question] was a confident 'Forward.' However fatuous and shallowly grounded may have been their faith that change meant progress, the Victorians were lucky they had it.'[39] In their belief that progress in the material sciences would be repeated in warfare, these officers were only guilty of articulating a specific example from the more general assumption. Again, as Altick says:

> Hope for the millennium was based on something called 'moral progress', the premise that human betterment was a built-in concomitant of material progress. By a happy Providence, cosmic tendency and the Victorians ambition coincided: the spirit of the universe [as we have seen, also formulated as the 'spirit' or 'intellect' of the age] was on their side.[40]

In his path-breaking *Voices Prophesying War 1763-1984* (1966), the historian of literature, I. F. Clarke, argued for much the same underlying belief system. In answering the question as to why concern for a future war preoccupied large numbers of popular fiction writers after 1871, he claimed that 'Technology was behind the whole process of advance as it was seen and felt by the Victorians'.[41] 'All the great advances from the steam engine and the railway to the laying of the Atlantic cable, the Suez canal, the cure of cholera', he added, 'all these had helped to convert the evident fact of change into the dogma of unending progress.'[42] If one needs a specific label for the Victorian military version of this conviction, then it can best be described as *British Victorian military millenarianism*. This articulated a firm conviction in the coming of an enlightened, scientific age where the few wars that would be fought between technologically advanced European powers would be fast, decisive and cheap. Yet, like most other writers before him, even Clarke makes the assumption that everyone in the British military at this time feared change. Like Bidwell, and echoing Fuller's thesis about the division between army and society, he argues that: 'Whilst a poet like Tennyson could find reasons for immense hope in the ringing groves of change, the admirals and the generals only too often could see nothing but disaster in the invention of the steam ship... The generation of the Reform Bill and the Great Exhibition had been born under the twin sign of Watt and Napoleon. Steam power and continental militarism appeared to make a nightmare of the future for many thoughtful people—especially for the military'.[43] While Naval planners may have worried, after mid-century, about the cost of replacing the old wooden fleet with a steam and iron one, it is something of an over-statement simply to assume that the Army worried about the steam engine. As this thesis now shows, the debate at the RUSI illustrates that, while there were certainly those who did not wish to consider change, and it is this group that provides the stereotype, many thinking British officers were deeply interested in the possibilities offered to them by the new technology. Military technology, therefore, provided the deterministic framework with which the millenarian military mind saw warfare and a higher moral order making progress hand in hand.[44]

One final observation about the RUSI's role in the promotion of this system of beliefs needs to be noted. How far the vision of future warfare articulated by those officers invited to give papers at the Institution actually reached into British political life can be gauged from the following remarks. On the eve of his famous reforms of the British Army in 1869, The Rt. Hon. Edward Cardwell, the Secretary of State for War, praised as his predecessors had done, the important new role of the institute. 'We live in a time when pure science, and applied science, and historical investigations', he said, 'contribute probably more than at any former period, to the real progress of the military profession.'[45]

> It is, therefore, peculiarly useful at the present time, that the most able and intellectual members of the two professions should have a home

> where they can meet in friendly intercourse and honourable rivalry, for the purpose of discussing questions relating to their professions. Their doing so ventilates those questions. Many of the most interesting subjects which afterwards occupy practical attention, find the first germs of their existence in the lectures of this institution; and according to what we read in the statements of modern philosophers, viz.; that germs when they are weakly, perish soon, and no more is heard of them, but that when they are hardy and robust, they flourish into the light: so those germs become the origin of future practical measure to be adopted by Government and State. Therefore it is that I feel not only the general advantage of the Institution, but its peculiar advantage at a period like the present.[46]

This high praise would have certainly delighted Lindsay. While members had aired their views on what would ultimately become Cardwell's famous plan for 'linking' the battalions of the British Army, the RUSI had been closely involved with the rifle question and had forged closer links with industrialists. All this practical activity between the organs of government and the army was clearly what the reformers had planned for in the previous decade. The deeper intellectual and informed opinion-shaping role of the body was also felt. In his conclusion, Cardwell, himself a former Colonel, spoke of the optimism that a civilian could feel in the scientific changes going on around them. Echoing what he had clearly learned from theorists such as Tyler, he concluded:

> [W]hen I read all that science is doing, the first thing that I rejoice in as a civilian, is to see that great as are the improvements in the arts of attack, if possible still greater are those which are made in the arts of defence. I trust that honourable rivalry will be maintained, and I for one shall always rejoice when I think that the science of defence is still gaining on the science of attack. The next remark I wish to make is this: a great philosopher has said that all things go round in cycles, and I have been extremely struck when I have noticed how very much progress of the most advanced science seems to bring us back upon the footprints of history. In the Middle Ages... men plated their bodies with

iron; we do not do this in our day, but we are all occupied in considering how best to plate our vessels with iron. Going back to a still earlier period, we find when Julius Caesar invaded England earthworks and entrenched camps were designed by the military science of that day; we find the most advanced science of modern days is carrying us back to the times of Caesar.[47]

Notes

1. J.Luvaas, *The Military Legacy of the Civil War: The European Inheritance*, (1988), p.14.
2. Luvaas considers this literature too, *ibid.*, pp. 14-30.
3. F.Miller, 'Military Sketch of the Present War in America', *JRUSI*, VI (1862), p.242.
4. *Ibid.*
5. *Ibid.*
6. *Ibid.*, p.260.
7. *Ibid.* While this clearly justified the British preference for a small professional army, it ignored the French experience from 1789 onwards of training recruits on the march. Miller argued wrongly that a 'change as would transform the Federal forces into a disciplined body must require a great space of time' (p.261). The only conclusion that Miller therefore reached about engagements rested on the observation that 'Whenever the opponents meet on neutral ground, the weaker in arms and numbers cannot fail to be worsted, unless, led by a superior skill which we can hardly expect to see' (p.262).
8. Luvaas, *op. cit.*, p.103.
9. C.C. Chesney, 'The Recent Campaigns in Virginia and Maryland', *JRUSI*, VII (1863), p.292.
10. Quoted in Luvaas, *op. cit.*, p.105.
11. Chesney, *op. cit.*, pp. 293-294.
12. *Ibid.*, p.293.
13. It is interesting to note that Luvaas says, for example, 'Few Englishmen thought that the American campaigns offered new lessons in strategy'. This is certainly true. However, Chesney *et al.*, did not formulate their arguments by using the term 'lessons'. Luvaas, *op. cit.*, (p.105).
14. H.W. Tyler, 'Railways Strategically Considered', *JRUSI*, VIII (1864),

p.321.
15. *Ibid.*, p.321.
16. *Ibid.*
17. *Ibid.*, pp. 321-322.
18. *Ibid.*, p. 322.
19. *Ibid.*, p.323.
20. *Ibid.* On a discussion of troops arriving at Turin he says: 'How different from the defenders of Sebastopol, who, from want of railway communication, lost the greater part of their number in crossing the steppes on their route to the scene of the conflict.' (p.326).
21. *Ibid.*, pp. 333-334.
22. *Ibid.*, p.334.
23. Luvaas, *op. cit.*, pp. 105-106.
24. Tyler, *op. cit.*, p.342.
25. *Ibid.*
26. Fuller, *op. cit.*, p.135.
27. *Ibid.*, p.136.
28. R. Altick, *Victorian People and Ideas*, (1973), p.98.
29. In his earlier remarks over what lay in store for nations that could not develop technological systems, Tyler was also expressing a deeply held moral feeling and vision about this change.
30. V. Majendie, 'The Martini-Henry Rifle', *JRUSI*, XIII (1869), p.379.
31. G.R. Burnell, 'On the Recent Progress of the Military Sciences', *JRUSI*, VII (1863), p. 395.
32. *Ibid.*, Lecture II, p.413.
33. G.V. Fosbury, 'On Mitrailleurs, and Their Place in the Wars of the Future', *JRUSI*, XIII (1869), p.539.
34. *Ibid.*, pp.539-540.
35. *Ibid.*, p.560.
36. *Ibid.*, p.562.
37. *Ibid.*
38. *Ibid.*
39. Altick, *op. cit.*, p.107.
40. *Ibid.*, p.108.
41. I.F. Clarke, *Voices Prophesying War 1763-1984*, (1966), pp.50-51.
42. *Ibid.*, p.51.

43. *Ibid.*, p.21.
44. To describe the influence of particular theological modes of thought on military behaviour would require a very different study than the one undertaken here. However, as the historian of science J. H. Brooke observes in *Science and Religion* (1991), 'A Protestant emphasis on improving the world, under the aegis of providence, could confer dignity on scientific activity that promised both glory to God and the relief of human suffering... Not withstanding the unbridled optimism of many such visions, it cannot be denied that one source of the modern idea of progress was this millenarian theology of puritan reformers anxious to transform the world in readiness for Christ's second coming.' (p.24). There is no reason to suppose that the gentlemen who filled the ranks of the officer corps were any less likely to make this leap (even if they were not conscious of it) than their counterparts in the clergy, law or academia.
45. E. Cardwell, 'Proceedings of the Thirty-ninth Anniversary Meeting', *JRUSI*, XIII (1870), p.x.
46. *Ibid.*
47. *Ibid.*